Never Give Up

TED JALETA'S INSPIRING STORY

To Carol
Live your dreams
Jaleta

Copyright © 2006 by JDC Productions
Ted Jaleta, Deana Driver and Peggy Collins

Second printing, 2006

All rights reserved. No part of this work may be reproduced or transmitted in any form or by any means – graphic, electronic or mechanic, including photocopying, recording, taping or information storage and retrieval systems – without the prior written permission of the publisher, or in the case of photocopying or other reprographic copying, a licence from the Canadian Copyright Licensing Agency.

Library and Archives Canada Cataloguing in Publication

Driver, Deana, 1956 -
NEVER GIVE UP: TED JALETA'S INSPIRING STORY / Deana Driver.
ISBN 0-9781341-0-9

1. Jaleta, Ted. 2. Runners (Sports)–Saskatchewan–Biography.
3. Motivational speakers–Saskatchewan–Biography.
4. Refugees–Ethiopia–Biography. 5. Refugees–Canada–Biography.
6. Motivation (Psychology). I. Title.

GV1061.15.J35D75 2006   796.42092   C2006-905198-4

Jacket photo: Greg Johnson
Jacket design: Jay Roach
Layout design: Deana Driver
Limited Edition Print: Tyson Kakakaway

Published by:
JDC Productions
3033 Victoria Avenue, Regina, Saskatchewan S4T 1L1 Canada

www.tedjaleta.com

Printed and bound in Canada

JDC Productions
gratefully acknowledges the financial assistance of the
Saskatchewan Publishers Group through the Cultural Industries
Development Fund

Never Give Up

TED JALETA'S INSPIRING STORY

* * *

Deana Driver

This book is dedicated to my beloved youngest sister Sadate, who helped me through difficult times in Ethiopia. Sadate died unnecessarily in 1993 from breast cancer. She was 31 years old.

– Ted Jaleta

Thousands of Canadians are touched by breast cancer every year. It impacts the people living with the disease, their families, friends and loved ones. The Canadian Breast Cancer Foundation is working to create a future without breast cancer by funding some of the most relevant breast cancer research programs in the country.

The foundation works collaboratively to fund, support and advocate for:
- *Relevant and innovative research,*
- *Meaningful education and awareness programs,*
- *Early diagnosis and effective treatment, and*
- *A positive quality of life for those living with breast cancer.*

JDC Productions is pleased to donate $1 from every NEVER GIVE UP *book sold to support the Canadian Breast Cancer Foundation*

Beautiful Things

The mountains threw a blanket over me,
As warm and protective as your love.
The moon and stars gave my way to see,
To deliver words protected from above.

I was young in purity,
Suffering my days in exile.
Running to a maturity,
Thinking beautiful things all the while.

My blood, my sister, my prayer,
The angel on my shoulder.
I thank you for being there,
Now I am older.

Did you know I would be here?
You knew good things must be.
Lost in a pain I used to fear,
The solution was always me.

So watch me from beautiful skies,
Free as a celestial bird, a dove.
Joy has returned to my eyes,
To you, I dedicate every word, with love.

By Tyson Kakakaway

(written for Ted Jaleta, in memory of his sister Sadate)

Contents

Part One

Prologue 11
Education is freedom 13
A new passion 26
Running for his life 34
Bruised but not beaten 41
Desperation 54
Light at the end of the tunnel 61

Part Two

Prologue Two 73
A new life 75
Second chance 91
Building momentum 101
Striving for excellence 117
Revisiting the past 127
A coach and leader 133
An honourable future 150

Epilogue 163

Notes 167
Acknowledgements 168

PART ONE

PROLOGUE

It's a warm summer day in 1991 and the hills of Banff, Alberta, Canada, are gloriously welcoming the 500 athletes who are running through this mountainside community in the annual Banff Road Race.

Ted Jaleta rounds the corner and heads further up into the hills. He has completed more than half of the 10-kilometre race and is near the front of the pack. His breath is laboured but he feels great.

Ted is happiest when he runs and he is enjoying these surroundings. The hills and mountains remind him of his birthplace in the high-altitude hills of northwestern Ethiopia, and his mind drifts back to his youth.

Ted sees himself running barefoot with his siblings and friends on narrow mountain paths and alongside streams and rivers. Laughing and playing as a small boy, these are among his most carefree days.

Then suddenly, Ted's mind reels with memories of his role in a peaceful protest. He sees people screaming and running everywhere, and his own blood on his pant leg.

Ted's thoughts suddenly shift again to a more pleasant recollection of time spent with his parents and neighbours around a community meal prepared by his mother. He recalls his mother's warm embrace and the approving nod of his father. Ted also remembers the incredible rush he felt when he won his first running competition at age 17 and was invited to join Ethiopia's national track team. He thinks back proudly of how he was the first in his farming family to get an education.

Those pleasant memories last only a few seconds. Then the nightmarish scenes return.

He sees himself, frightened and bruised, in an Ethiopian prison. Then he's running for his life. Away from the prison, from his family and Ethiopia, the only land he ever knew. He remembers the squalor of a refugee camp and struggling to get enough to eat. Those thoughts make him shudder.

Then Ted rounds a corner of the road in Banff and the cheers of the crowd snap him back into the present day, waking him from his daydream.

He's in Canada now. He's winning the race. And he's safe.

It will all be okay.

CHAPTER ONE

EDUCATION IS FREEDOM

The rainy season in the northwestern part of the Ethiopian Highlands was almost at an end. The daytime temperature was slowly climbing from the winter average of 5 degrees Celsius towards the summer high of about 30 degrees. Although the country of Ethiopia would later be etched in the memories of many North Americans for its widespread drought and famine beginning in the early 1970s, this was not the scene on the hills west of Lake Tana on September 24, 1954. The land here was rich with vegetation and the farmers looked forward to another year of good crops.

Ethiopia covers about one million square kilometres on the northeastern tip of the continent of Africa. The elevation in this part of the Ethiopian Highlands is about 1,300 metres (4,000 feet) above sea level, less than half the altitude of Ethiopia's capital city of Addis Ababa hundreds of kilometres to the south.

The view from this village of 500 residents is similar to what one would see looking at the forests and foothills in parts of the Rocky Mountains in North America. The cliffs, rocky spires and mountains of the highlands give Ethiopia its nickname of 'The Roof of Africa.'

The small grass-roofed huts made of wood and mudded bamboo dot the farming plateau here in clumps of two or three. Most families have a main home plus a hut for their guests and one for their older children. In 1954, the buildings that belonged to Didi Jaleta and his wife Tobias Abate sat on the edge of the village.

The Jaletas were among the wealthiest farmers in the community and owned another hut about a half-hour walk from the closest farm. This is where they kept their several hundred cattle, sheep, goats and chickens, far away from the other people of the village. They also had another hut located about an hour's walk down the hill in a cattle-grazing area.

Monkeys and gelada baboons roamed freely on the hills around the village, sharing the land with their human neighbours. The creatures chattered loudly on this day, but their noisy bantering was not enough to distract from what was happening inside the Jaletas' main house.

There, the small-framed Tobias was on a simple bed, writhing in pain, struggling to give birth. There was no doctor or hospital nearby and the local midwife who was helping Tobias was fearful because the birth was not going well. She was worried for Tobias and for the health of the baby.

Tobias continued to struggle and many nerve-wracking hours later, Didi was relieved to watch his wife give birth to their fourth child, who weighed a strapping nine pounds. Didi was sure the baby, their second son, would grow to be a big help on the farm.

The jubilation surrounding the boy's arrival did not last for long, though. Tobias was very ill. Shortly after the baby was born, she lapsed into a coma.

The newborn son was sent to a nursemaid in the village while family members spent the next few days at Tobias' bedside, watching, waiting and hoping that she would somehow recover.

Amazingly, after more than a week, Tobias came out of the coma. It was a miracle, celebrated by the whole community that year and every year afterwards on the date of that baby's birth.

Shortly after Tobias recovered, the baby was returned to the family home and given a name. They called him Tewodros (Ted) Jaleta after Emperor Tewodros II who had tried to reunify the regional kings and warlords who ruled Ethiopia in 1855.

That emperor's desire to bring people together would later become a characteristic of Ted Jaleta's own existence. His namesake, in some small way, might also have encouraged Ted to stay on his own path to greatness so many years later.

* * *

For the first few years of Ted's life, his days were carefree. He enjoyed running barefoot on the narrow mountain paths near his family's home, playing with his older sisters and brother, and sleeping in the main house on a wooden cot or an animal-skin rug on the floor. He visited his mother's family, who lived in the same community, and particularly loved the scenery surrounding his home.

Evergreen, bamboo, juniper, acacia, olive and fig trees were everywhere. The scent of fragrant eucalyptus trees and giant lobelia flowers filled his nostrils during the summer. There were bees' nests to explore and wild blueberries, strawberries and plums to taste. It was a great place to play as a child.

Ted liked to daydream while looking at the hills and mountains, but he was always brought back to reality by the colonies of monkeys and baboons playing and chattering at all hours. The white-bearded colobus monkeys were his favourite. They spend most of their time in the trees and are very peaceful animals.

Hyenas were also common in the Ethiopian Highlands but Ted and his friends tried to avoid these annoying, noisy scavengers who could carry a variety of diseases. There were wolves and cheetahs in the highlands as well, but these creatures usually avoided contact with humans.

Lack of food was never a concern for Ted or his family. His parents grew coffee, lentils, potatoes, beans, bananas, papayas and more. When Ted was a child, the soil in the highlands was rich and the climate was perfect for almost any crop. Occasionally, the Jaletas shared some of their food with friends, relatives and neighbours who might not have access to milk or meat as they did.

Ted's father was also a shrewd businessman who purchased items such as salt, sugar and clothing from merchants who passed through the village. He then sold these products to the local people for a small profit.

When Ted was a child, weekends were a time of neighbourhood get-togethers. Villagers took turns hosting the gatherings in their own homes. The hosts would brew coffee, the country's main export, and share it with their guests. The adults sat in a circle and visited. They nibbled on bread and drank their strong coffee from cups that are smaller than North American teacups.

Ted loved these gatherings, where he drank milk or tea with the other children and played games like soccer, hide-and-seek, and checkers or backgammon using seeds or pebbles, while the parents visited. It was a very happy childhood.

Of course, it wasn't much by North American standards but it was more than enough for a young African boy who to this day knows that he can survive on very little.

Ted's family spent the winter rainy season from June to October at their home in the highlands, away from the swelling rivers and streams and the pesky mosquitoes and leeches of the lowlands. During the dry season from November to May, Ted's father and some helpers moved down from the steep hills to the grasslands area to take the livestock to pasture. The rest of the family stayed behind except to occasionally take the men some dry goods and to visit. It was a half-day walk to take the animals down from the mountains to a good pasture area.

In those days, land in the northern and western parts of Ethiopia was open for any farmer to use for their animals to graze. Land in most of the rest of the country was not. It was owned by Ethiopia's royal family and by nobles who were loyal to the royal family. That ownership would become a huge issue in the country when Ted was older.

"Peasants made up the majority of Ethiopia's population and yet they owned little or no land. They were only allowed to be tenants of the land. This caused a lot of despair and resentment among the peasants."

Of course, Ted was still years away from having that discussion. He took pleasure in the simple, stress-free days of childhood. There was nothing to fear.

Until school began.

* * *

Orthodox Christianity and the monarchy had their beginnings in Ethiopia in the 4th century A.D., and were the two dominant powers in Ethiopia when Ted was young. The Orthodox Church at one time is believed to have owned one-third of the country's land.[1]

In the 1950s and 1960s, schools were opened in Ted's region of the country. Orthodox Christians were responsible for bringing religion to the 'uneducated' peasants and teaching religion as part of the school curriculum, mostly to boys. Girls were not encouraged to go to school. Their roles were in the home, learning to be good housewives for their future husbands.

Ted and his older brother were the first generation of their family to attend school. Although Ted was excited to leave the painful manual labour of the farm, he was also sad that he would be away from his mother and sisters during the day. He knew he would have to run about 10 kilometres with the boys of his village to get to the nearest grade school. There would be no chance of support from their families if anything happened at school or along the way. He didn't know what would happen once he started classes, but he knew it would probably not be easy.

Running barefoot for long distances through the mountains, or anywhere else for that matter, is a ridiculous idea to most modern-day North Americans. But it has been a normal way of life for generations of people in Africa. As well as being the only method of transportation available in most Ethiopian communities when Ted was young, the simple act of running encouraged a lifestyle of fitness and led to the crowning of many of the world's greatest long distance runners.

The trip to school took 45 minutes to an hour, depending on how the boys felt and how fast they ran on any given day. "We ran hard and when we got tired, we sat down and recovered and then ran again," Ted recalls.

Ted and his friends would sometimes stop to rest or have a drink of water at a mountain stream or creek. Occasionally, they would snack on non-perishable foods like roasted salted grain or chickpeas that their mothers had put in their knapsacks, or on wild berries they found along the way. If they were really hungry, they got an early start on the lunches they carried, which included pieces of crepe-like bread that was either buttered or wrapped around beans like a pita. They would rarely have a banana or other piece of fruit in their bags for dessert because fruit would not have travelled well on the back of a small running child.

After a short rest beside the stream, the boys would be off running again. "When we got to school, we were all dripping with sweat. It was normal," explains Ted.

The school in those days was a simple, sparsely furnished hut. There might have been a wooden bench for the students but Ted mostly remembers sitting on the dirt floor, watching the teacher with wide eyes and considerable fear.

A common practice in schools throughout much of the world in those days was to punish students for being late for class or for not learning their lessons. Ted and the other children were often strapped for their tardiness. Most of the time their lateness was due to having helped on the farm in the mornings before going to school. After Ted woke at five or six o'clock every morning, he was expected to help milk cows, move the animals from one penned area to another, or help with the food crops. Ted also had to gather the dried cow dung into piles so it could be burned to make a good fertilizer for future crops.

The process for planting crops involved cutting bamboo trees in the spring with an axe or knife and collecting the cut pieces into piles to be burned. The ashes served as fertilizer and were sometimes tilled into the soil with a plow that was pulled by a horse or ox. Corn and other crops were then planted by hand. Ted remembers the callouses on his hands from working so hard. After a couple years, the bamboo grew tall and the process of cutting and burning started again.

Going to school was much more appealing to Ted than working on the farm, but he hated being late for classes and the punishment that came with it. How was he supposed to know when it was time to go to school? There were no clocks in his community. "We didn't have any concept of time. We didn't have watches. We looked at the sun and guessed."

Ethiopia has a unique way of telling time. Days begin at sunrise, which does not vary much throughout the year because Ethiopia is close to the equator. Dawn arrives at 1 a.m. and the day ends at 12:59 a.m. September is the first month of the Ethiopian year. The country also uses the Julian calendar of 12 months of 30 days plus a 13th month of five days, or six days in a leap year.[2] The Ethiopian calendar is seven years and eight months behind the Gregorian calendar used in most Western countries so Ted's birth certificate, if one had been issued in those days, would say he was born in 1947 instead of 1954. While Ethiopian businesses that deal with other countries have adapted to Western culture time-wise, many rural communities continue with the traditional patterns.

But Ted knew none of this when he was younger. At the time, the most important thing to him was the certain knowledge that he would be in trouble if he arrived late for class. So he was thrilled when, a couple years after he started school, his father brought a shortwave radio home from a trip to Sudan. One morning when they heard the time announced on the radio, the boys measured the shadow of a tree and used that measurement from then on as the indication of when it was time to leave home.

In Ted's eyes, the abuse for being late to school was difficult, but even worse was the punishment he received for speaking his mother tongue. This transgression was harder to understand and it left a long-standing mark on young Ted that would drive him to improve himself and help others for many years to come.

Ted's family was Boro, a minority group in Ethiopia which was often ridiculed as being uneducated and uncivilized. Most of the adults and leaders in the country at that time were from the dominant Amhara ethnic group, and children in school were supposed to learn and use only the written and spoken Amharic language.

The Boro people had been given a derogatory name by the Amhara. "They called us Shinasha," Ted remembers, still feeling the sting of those insults. "It has negative connotations. We prefer to be called Boro after the language we speak." More than 80 languages are spoken in Ethiopia today and many of these languages, including Ted's mother tongue, are oral languages only.

Ethiopia is the only country in Africa that has never been fully colonized by Europeans. This is why Ethiopia is the only African country that has developed its own alphabet, the Amharic alphabet.

Ted's first year of grade school was particularly challenging and frustrating because of the problems he had in learning the new language. "We were all forced to memorize the alphabet, make a sentence and understand the meaning of it. It wasn't my mother tongue and I was having difficulty. At the time, I was called stupid."

Ted remembers being summoned to the front of the class on several occasions to be strapped for not properly learning Amharic. "It was humiliating."

At one point, he was so frustrated by this intimidation that he ran to school each morning with the other boys of his village but spent the entire week hiding in the bushes instead of going into the school. His mother eventually found out what he was doing and told him he had to go back to class.

He told his mother: "I can't go to school. I will get punished." But his mother was insistent. She promised that she would talk to the teacher so he would not be disciplined again. So Ted reluctantly went back to class.

Despite his mother's efforts, Ted was called to the front of the room that first day back. But before the teacher could do much else, Ted took off running.

He headed towards home, trying to outrun the pain and humiliation of the strap. The teacher ordered the other students to chase Ted and bring him back to the classroom, so there were at least 100 children running after Ted down the dirt path. Then the teacher joined the pursuit.

Ted was faster than most of the other students. And he was scared.

He knew if they caught him, he would be punished. If he got away, he would be punished later, but he didn't care. He had to try to get home to where his mother could save him.

After several minutes, the children trailed off and soon only the teacher remained in the chase. Stronger legs and more stamina brought the teacher within reach after about 10 more minutes of hard, desperate running. Young Ted paid a dear price for his attempted escape.

"I was whipped with a stick and hit across the face. My lips were cut. My face was bleeding."

After school, Ted went to his grandmother's house instead of home. "If I had the power to disappear somewhere that day, I would have, but I couldn't. I felt betrayed by my mother and I didn't think my dad would care. My grandma fed me and comforted me. Then she sent me home."

Ted went to school the following day, this time with a new purpose. In his young mind, he thought he would teach his mother a lesson for making him go back. "She'll miss me when I'm at school and she'll be crying," he said to himself. Of course, that wasn't logical to anyone but Ted at the time, but it was enough motivation to keep him at school for the next while.

Years later, Ted learned that his mother had also been devastated by the treatment he had experienced at school that day. She had cried and been terribly upset that he had been punished when she had assured him it would not happen.

"What could she do?" says Ted, looking back. "Things got easier after that. When I reached Grade 3, I mastered the language."

He is now glad that his mother made him return to classes. "If she had said: 'Oh, my poor son,' and kept me home, I don't think I would have pursued my education."

Shortly after that first major disagreement with his teacher, Ted decided not to let challenges in his life weigh him down. Although he ran away on that day, he has since stood up to most obstacles in his path and has used his brains instead of brawn to win battles and improve his life.

"When I was younger, I used to get bullied and I didn't like it. One time, I organized my own defensive group of kids."

Ted and his friends hid in the bushes and jumped on the ringleader of the group that had been picking on them. They demanded he give them a ride on his back from one point to another. He begged them for mercy and they released him after he promised not to pick on them anymore. That small victory did not mean the struggles with that boy were over, however. They were just fewer and farther apart.

"We knew to always stick together because if he found one of us alone, we were dead meat," Ted laughs.

Ted's determination to achieve was obvious even from that age. "Many kids couldn't handle the bullying and went back to the farm. I decided I was not going to do that. I needed education." Ted became one of the top students in the class from Grade 3 on, but there were always reminders that he and his friends were not in the majority.

Children at school teased Ted and his Boro friends and said negative things about his ethnic group. These kinds of statements pushed Ted even further in his desire to show them his true skills and abilities. He wasn't about to let their taunting get the best of him.

"When people called me names, I never felt less than them," he says of his experiences in childhood and throughout the rest of his life. "That is learned behaviour. And it can happen anywhere in the world. Some of the kids from ethnic minorities in Canada have told me they get picked on by other students."

Ted has a message for those kids – and anyone else who encounters difficult times: "Do not dwell on the negative and do not be deterred by the challenges you face. You have to work hard and believe in yourself."

* * *

When Ted was in Grade 2, his older brother died. The boy had been sick for a couple of weeks and his condition gradually worsened until he went into a coma a few days before he died. Ted isn't even sure what caused the illness. "It could have been a simple infection. It could have been malaria or anything."

There were no hospitals or doctors in that region of Ethiopia in those days and death from illness was common. It was a traumatic event for Ted. It was the first time he had witnessed the death of a close family member. He was sad at the loss of his big brother and all the fun they would never have together. Ted's brother had been the first person in the family to learn how to read and write. He had taught Ted so much.

Ted realized later that his brother's death was also hard because it was the first time he was faced with his own mortality, and he had the added pressure of becoming the oldest boy in the family. Ted's parents expected much more from him on the farm after that.

When he was 10 years old, Ted had to go to a new school farther away, walking for three days with the other boys of his village to a nearby city where he could take Grade 4 to Grade 8 classes. The walk took the group down from the hills into the semi-arid lowlands, across a couple of rivers and up into the hills again. The boys travelled with two of their fathers, who helped the younger children across the still-swollen rivers and got them safely to the school. By the time Ted was in Grade 7, he was big enough that he could make these long trips to school himself with just a couple friends.

A week or so before Ted left for Grade 4 on the first of those three-day journeys, he noticed a change in the atmosphere of his home. His sisters were more sullen and his mother would occasionally burst into tears when she looked at him. He was, after all, the oldest son now, and would be going away for months at a time, coming home only for Christmas, Easter and the busy winter break of July and August when most of the work is done on the farm. Ted's older brother had never had the opportunity of attending this school before he died, and it would be quite a change in the Jaleta home to have a child gone for so long.

Ted's parents and some other families in his village had rented a large house in the city and hired a nanny to look after Ted and the other children during the school year. At this home-away-from-home, Ted was expected only to occasionally cut trees and bring the pieces back for firewood. Although Ted was happy to leave the hard farm work behind, he was already lonely for his family, especially his mother. He would miss her love and support, and her meals. After all, no one's food was as good as his mother's cooking.

For the long journey, the children wore their usual outfits of shorts and a shirt, and carried a change of clothing in their knapsacks, including pants and simple, hand-made sandals. If they needed new clothes while at school, their families were contacted via travelling merchants to send money to pay a local tailor to make the items.

The group walked along together, with a donkey or mule carrying enough dry food supplies for the children for a few months at a time. If the students ran low on staple foods while at school, they sent word with the merchants that they needed their parents to send more salt, honey, potatoes or other items. It was a system that worked well for all of Ted's school years.

With daytime temperatures as high as 30 degrees Celsius, the travellers occasionally rested under the trees by a river during the day and walked at night when the temperature was a more comfortable 15 degrees. It was peaceful to walk by moonlight.

At some midday stops, the children enjoyed fishing and swimming in the cold water of the streams. The water was so clean in some areas that they could see fish swim by. The boys jumped in and tried to grab the fish, but were usually more successful in spearing them, to later cook over the campfire.

The trips to and from this new school are among the most joyous memories Ted has of his childhood. "My happiest times growing up were with nature. In June, when everything was green and the flowers were blooming, I would sit in the calmness and listen to the incredible noises of birds and bees. Every creature was busy capturing that moment in time to do its work. It was just beautiful."

As the children travelled to school, they saw orioles, finches and crows. Sometimes, Ted would take a nap under the trees along a river's edge or just play on the sandy beaches. He and his friends also hunted for the honeycombs of wild bees or followed a local bird that led them to the sweet treat.

In the lowlands, the children passed large termite mounds, sand dunes, bamboo trees and various reeds and grasses that grew three times the size of an adult man. They saw poisonous snakes, spiny-tailed lizards, chameleons, gazelles, monkeys and baboons in those grasslands. Occasionally, they'd also see lions, which stayed away from humans most times and could be kept away at night with a campfire. The group slept on beds of leaves they made on the forest floor. On some nights, Ted watched the bats fly overhead. He recalls sitting by a river on several quiet black nights, watching the bright signals of lightning bugs reflect on the water.

During his months away from the farm and his village, Ted became even more convinced that going to school would provide the best future for him. "Education gives you freedom and knowledge. In my ethnic minority, there were very few people who knew how to read and write. When anyone from our village wanted to write a letter, they had to go to the proper business people who wrote the letter and charged for their services. We were looked down on because we were uneducated. That really bothered me when I was a child."

Ted saw the higher standard of living of the educated administrators and leaders who came to the village. These were the people elected into Parliament. They were the ones with professional training and a paid salary. They didn't have to work on the farm, and had nice clothes and many other things that Ted and his family didn't have. As a child, Ted wanted to be one of those people and have their opportunities.

When Ted was 13 years old, a horrifying incident further cemented his desire for a better future away from the farm. It also instilled his life-long passion of encouraging both women and men in Africa and around the world to pursue higher learning.

According to the tradition of those times, Ethiopian parents arranged marriages for their teenaged daughters, often in an effort to improve the bride's social status and future. Ted's father had approved such a marriage for his 15-year-old daughter. But she didn't want to marry the proposed groom, who was quite a bit older than her, and she ran away the night before the wedding. When the groom-to-be arrived on horseback the next day to collect his bride, Ted's father sent his 11-year-old daughter, kicking and screaming, in place of the older sister to fulfill his part of the agreement.

The next day, an uncle found the older sister hiding in the mountains and tried to bring her back to the farm. The girl bolted from the uncle and jumped off a cliff, committing suicide.

"It was horrible to watch my younger sister be dragged away," Ted remembers. "It was sad. We lost two sisters from our home in two days. Living with our father afterwards with that memory wasn't easy. Some of us took a long time to forgive my dad for that. We rarely discussed it."

Ted was also confused, upset and even angry with his older sister for her decision to commit suicide rather than marry. "Disobeying and going as far as killing herself, what was she thinking?"

Ted's father never again approved such a marriage arrangement and it was a long time before any of the wounds healed. They simply had to live through it. For Ted, it wasn't as bad because he was away at school a lot. "It was hard on both my parents. My dad believed he was right in making the decisions without consulting my mother. He was also unhappy my sister disobeyed him and sad that she died. For my mom, the pain of losing two daughters was very tough. She and my dad almost split up."

Ted sometimes wonders what might have happened if his sisters had been encouraged to go to school as he did. What would their lives have been like? Gender inequality is very common in Ethiopia and Ted believes that education is the key to narrowing the gender gap. "Education can help women avoid being subject to abuse or control."

Ethiopia is not alone in the need to bridge this gap, he adds. "Prior to the Second World War, most North American women were homemakers.

There were not many in power positions and few had an opportunity to pursue a post-secondary education. Divorce rates at the time were minimal. The reason those women were trapped in unhealthy relationships was because the breadwinners at the time were men. Now women don't have to put up with that. They are breadwinners, too. They are educated, and that has given them more freedom. It has not been handed to them. They earned it."

Equal to Ted's determination to encourage higher learning is his commitment to encourage proper use of that valuable resource.

"Canadian children tend to take such a privilege as going to school for granted. Even all the extra curricular activities they get such as sports, music, etc. are extreme gifts when compared to what is received by the children of Ethiopia."

Everyone, male and female, can take advantage of the gift of education and use it to improve their lives. It may not come easily, but it is worth the struggle.

Chapter Two

A New Passion

Ted may have wanted an education and a life away from the farm, but his father had other ideas. When Ted reached Grade 6, his dad tried to keep him home and refused to give him supplies or money for school.

Ted had already been forced to miss a few days of classes to help with the harvest when he was younger. He wasn't keen on staying home permanently, so he came up with a plan that he thought would allow him to stay in school.

He had his own beehives and tried to sell the honey he collected to provide funds for his education. His dad saw through that scheme and confiscated Ted's money, saying all income earned now had to go into the family's general revenue. Ted and his father had a huge fight about this arbitrary decision and, in the end, Ted ignored his father's wishes and travelled to school as usual with his neighbourhood friends. Ted's mother hadn't been able to convince him to stay home, either. Rather than see her son suffer, she packed Ted some snacks for the road and gave him a bit of cash for some school supplies, against the wishes of her husband. Ted had to be careful with his money from that point on and sometimes relied on the generosity of other students who shared their food with him.

The summer that Ted completed Grade 8, both of his parents told him that he was finished with school. He was now expected to stay home and work on the farm. He was devastated.

"My parents said: 'You are done. You know how to read and write.

Now you have to take charge of the farm. We need you here.' At the time, having many children provided a labour force for them, so they needed me at home," Ted recalls. His parents would eventually have nine children.

Although Ted understood the importance of keeping the farm going, he couldn't accept his parents' decision about his own future. The nearest school for subsequent grade levels was located even farther away from home and getting to school would be an even bigger challenge than it had been already. He was confused and depressed and didn't know what to do.

Ted told his older sister he was considering moving in with an uncle who lived in a different province where there was a high school. It is an Ethiopian custom to take care of family members of the younger generation, and the uncle had quietly offered to help Ted financially if he wanted to continue his schooling.

After much anguish and without telling his parents, Ted made up his mind. He had to run away from home.

But first, Ted needed some money to travel to where his uncle lived. He had seen his parents bury some of their hard-earned cash in a clay pot in the yard. No one trusted banks at that time and the banks were too far away from the village anyway. When nobody was looking, Ted dug up the clay pot and grabbed some cash out of it.

The money in the pot was covered in ash to prevent termites from getting at it, but the ash wasn't completely successful in doing its job. There were holes in the money bills. "The termites somehow got in!" Ted laughs, as he remembers being able to see light shine through some of the bills. That discovery provided a brief moment of humour at the beginning of what was otherwise a gut-wrenching escapade.

"I took money from my parents without their permission and I left without the approval of my mom and dad." While Ted still regrets stealing from his family, he doesn't regret his decision to leave home.

"I knew there was a greater purpose to my life than just working on the farm. Education would be the key to my freedom." It was a huge decision for a 14-year-old to make but Ted was sure it would be worth the effort and he would be able to endure whatever difficulties came with his decision.

Ted left home just before daylight the next morning and walked for two and a half days down from the mountains through the tall grasses and reeds to the nearest city. He paid for a ride on a lorry truck that was delivering goods south to the city of Debre Mark'os and then took a bus from there to the capital city of Addis Ababa and caught a train heading east across Ethiopia. On the sixth day after he'd left home, Ted reached the city of Harer where his uncle lived.

Ted's parents somehow found out about their son's plans, likely from his sister, and his uncle received a message from Ted's father shortly after the boy arrived. "My uncle was very concerned," recalls Ted. "My dad was very vocal and was displeased with me. At the time, my dad said he was going to disown me." His father's wrath could have caused trouble for Ted's uncle within the family, and his uncle worried about the consequences of providing Ted a refuge.

"In my culture, if you do not listen to your parents, you're seen as a bad person," explains Ted. "I had taken that chance. If I had done poorly in school, it would have been said that I deserved it because I disobeyed my dad."

That concern wasn't an issue for long, as Ted continued to excel in school and became more involved in visible roles such as the debating club and student council.

* * *

Soccer and volleyball were the most common sports for Ethiopian children to take part in at that time and Ted, like most of his friends, wanted to become a major soccer star who was idolized by the entire country. When he was in Grades 8 and 9, he played in a loosely-organized soccer league away from school, but he had more heart for the game than he had talent.

"I was a benchwarmer. I was quite fast but I was too skinny, so I got pushed to the ground a lot. Sometimes I would pray that somebody would get injured so I could play. Most of the time, my prayers were not answered," he says with a sheepish grin. "The idea of being a soccer star and being good at it are totally different. I tried so hard. My heart was there. I thought I was good, but I wasn't."

Track and cross-country running were in the physical education curriculum at the time, and Ted would do what was required and run along with the rest of the class. Barefoot, of course.

"I got my first pair of shoes when I was in Grade 5 or 6 but I didn't use them very often. Shoes were just for when I went to church or to look good. I didn't want my shoes to wear out."

In about Grade 9, a teacher approached Ted and decided that he was in the wrong sport. The teacher was in charge of the boys' running team and told Ted that he could be a good runner instead of a soccer player. The teacher then made a pronouncement that changed Ted's life forever. "You are running," he stated.

Ted finished third in his first track meet and won his next race. After seeing his name in the newspaper, he started to think more seriously about a possible future as a runner.

The idea took a stronger hold in Grade 10 when Abebe Bikila, Ethiopia's celebrated two-time Olympic gold medallist, visited the school on a tour of the country. Bikila, the legendary 'barefoot runner' who won the Olympic marathon in 1960 and 1964, spoke to the students about the importance of education, hard work and hope – concepts that Ted still embraces.

"He made me believe in myself. Bikila's message was to make the right choices, to work hard and not set barriers. His message was engraved in my head and remains with me to this day. It was so powerful and clear," says Ted, his face still lighting up at the memory of that day.

Up until that point in Ted's life, his teachers had told him he could be a better runner than he was already. Bikila's message reinforced that position. It made him realize that running was one of the things he could be good at and able to pursue in the future.

Olympians are heroes in Ethiopia. They are more popular than the prime minister and are often honoured with statues in the national stadium. Ted longed to be one of those champions.

Bikila is an Ethiopian running legend in a country and continent that expects its celebrated athletes to give back to the community and share their wisdom and wealth. These are lessons that Ted learned well from Bikila and went on to emulate in later years. From Bikila, Ted also learned the right reasons for running. 'Don't do it because you want to be glorified. Do it because you love it, and the glory, winning and rewards will come by themselves,' the legendary runner told the students.

Today, decades later, when Ted runs either in a race or for fitness, Bikila often travels with him in spirit. "I still can visualize him when I'm running. I see him running beside me. I am grateful to Abebe for giving me that light, that insight."

At the end of Grade 10, Ted's father paid a visit to his eldest son. He was no longer angry with the boy for leaving home, because he had heard good reports of the teenager's school activities. "They knew I was doing well. Dad was pleased to see me. He hugged me and cried. I knew he wanted to apologize."

But Ted hadn't needed to hear those words from his father. The fact that his dad had come to visit was enough to convince Ted to go home for the winter break. The following year, Ted started Grade 11 in the city of Debre Mark'os, much closer to the family's home.

Ted worked on the farm during his breaks from school, but also used his knowledge to help educate others in the village. Police and court officials asked him to translate for local citizens from their own language to Amharic. Ted willingly volunteered his services. "I felt I needed to advocate for them because they didn't understand the language. I didn't want others to take advantage of them." The villagers appreciated his efforts, paid him with a meal and praised him for his literacy skills.

When Ted was home, he also taught several local peasants how to read and write. Less than 10% of Ethiopia's population was literate at the time and Ted felt compelled to do his part to improve those statistics.[3] "I would attach a blackboard to a tree trunk and teach them while they sat in the shade."

* * *

Every year in high school, there were competitions for spots on the high school track team. Ted had not tried too hard to win these events in Grades 9 and 10 because he was still more interested in being a soccer star. But in 1972, near the end of Grade 11, his running skills had improved enough that he placed third locally and advanced to the regional competition. He knew if he won the regionals, he would receive a highly-coveted free trip to the capital city for the national championship. It meant he would travel by bus to Addis Ababa, stay in a dorm and, more importantly, be given a souvenir T-shirt of the event. Ted was determined to run as fast as he could to get that trip.

So he trained harder and won the regional race with a convincing victory. He was thrilled to be going to the nationals, just for the fun of it. But once he got to the national junior-age high school 10-kilometre (10K) championship race in Addis Ababa, Ted's emotions alternated between awe, uncertainty and fear.

The stadium in the centre of the capital city was the largest one Ted had ever been in. He had seen people playing soccer there before, but had never been on the track himself. Ted remembers the beautiful blue sky that day and the thousands of spectators who crammed in to watch this much-anticipated race. It was standing room only and spectators were even perched in the trees outside the stadium.

The sun was about to set and the temperature must have been about 20 degrees Celsius, but Ted was too excited and overwhelmed to think about the weather for long.

He was the underdog and was only there because he had won the regional championships. Being an underdog meant Ted didn't have any pressure to win, so he could take a moment to savour the experience. "I was just glad to be there. I didn't have any particular strategy on how to race. I was inexperienced. At the time, I was only planning to follow the leaders."

It didn't turn out that way, though.

As the race progressed, Ted was in the second pack of runners. "As we approached the halfway point, I started closing in on the front runners and I sensed the fatigue in them. With a few laps remaining, the crowd was going crazy to encourage the leaders, and I was getting closer and closer to the front. I finally caught them with about a lap and a half to go and I just stayed behind them."

Running at the front of a pack and setting the pace is mentally and physically exhausting. The runners who are behind the leader will often stay there and watch for a moment of weakness in the leader so they can take advantage of it and burst forward to win. That is exactly what Ted did in this national juniors' race.

"I used them for another half a lap and then I dared to go," he says. "I just ran scared. I thought those runners were going to catch me because, in my mind, they were better than me."

It was an idea fostered by fear and inexperience, but Ted really had no reason to worry. He won the race, coming in a full 50 metres in front of the second-place runner.

"When I crossed the finish line, I couldn't believe it," he says. "I thought: 'Is this a dream?' It was an unbelievable feeling. I was crying. I felt so much joy!"

His winning time of 30 minutes, 30 seconds was excellent for a high altitude where less oxygen is available. At sea level, Ted's time likely would have been at least a minute and a half faster.

One of the teenagers Ted beat in that race was Mohamed Kedir, who went on to win the bronze medal for Ethiopia in the 10K race at the 1980 Moscow Olympics. But Ted wasn't thinking much about those who came behind him that day. The only things that mattered to him at the end of that race were getting his first-place ribbon and enjoying his victory.

What a sweet victory it was, and it became even better when it was time for Ted to collect his prize. The person on the podium who handed him his ribbon and shook his hand was none other than his hero, Abebe Bikila.

"It was like meeting the emperor," says Ted, still awestruck by the memory. Bikila was paralyzed and in a wheelchair as a result of a car accident. He died the following year.

Another important moment in Ted's life occurred that same day when shortly after the race, an official from the Ethiopian Track and Field Federation invited him to join the national track team. This would give him the potential to be a high-calibre runner representing the country, and perhaps even lead to the Olympic Games.

The invitation was an incredible gift to a novice runner like Ted. It would be the Canadian equivalent of being a National Hockey League prospect. He was hopeful about the possibility of becoming an Olympian, though he knew there were no guarantees.

"There are many good junior hockey players in Canada. How many of them make the NHL? Very few. I told them I was not yet ready to join the team until I finished Grade 12. At the time, my focus was education. My thinking was I didn't want running to control my life. Running is from one point to another. Eventually you get there. I had to think about what I would do after running."

It's a lesson that Ted has passed on to each and every young athlete he has met since.

The following year was full of promise for Ted. He completed Grade 11 and entered Grade 12 full of optimism for his life after high school. He achieved good grades and was active in school politics. He'd been the president of the student council in Grade 11 and was editor of the high-profile student newspaper in Grade 12. Things couldn't get much better.

"My future looked bright. In Ethiopia, if you are a high-calibre runner, they usually make you join the army or the police force if you are not getting a post-secondary education. You do not necessarily do the duty, but you stay on the payroll. Bikila himself was a member of the Imperial guard."

Ted was not interested in being in the military, though. Instead, he wanted to run while attending university. Universities are free to those who attain the required scholastic marks in Ethiopia. Ted was anxious to train to become a doctor or learn a similar profession that could improve his life and those of the people around him. Meanwhile, he could work towards achieving his Olympic dream in a sport that was loved by everyone in his country.

"I am the kind of person who would have capitalized on that, but I didn't get that opportunity."

Ted's world was about to change dramatically. His dreams would soon be crushed.

Chapter Three

Running For His Life

Haile Selassie was emperor of Ethiopia from 1930 through to Ted's high school years, becoming the country's last and longest-ruling emperor. Selassie made a number of improvements to Ethiopia's economic and social conditions during his reign, including expanding the modern school system and the police force,[4] but he always faced opposition.

Ethiopia's economic conditions worsened after 1968, partly due to a decline in the price of coffee and the closing of the Suez Canal, which stalled exports and imports.[5] Drought, famine and inflation caused added strain, and the educated class began to have less success in obtaining government jobs. University students demonstrated and organized campaigns against both the government and various merchants who were raising food prices.[6]

Troubled times increased for the emperor in the early 1970s after a documentary by British Broadcasting Corporation journalist Jonathan Dimbleby focused the world's attention on the widespread famine in the Wollo province and Haile Selassie's refusal to recognize and address that problem.[7] This made Ethiopians more eager than ever to bring down the monarchy and spur on democratic reform.

By this time, students and other intellectuals wanted reforms to the land ownership rules that kept farms in the hands of the powerful and away from the starving peasants. Teachers, educated workers and members of the country's military all wanted better pay and better working conditions. They wanted elections and a voice in the country's future.

When Ted was in Grade 12, he often used his school newspaper editorials to support the growing movement for reform. Lack of elections, gender inequality and separation of church and state were burning issues for him and other students. As the newspaper editor, Ted spoke up for freedom of religion and freedom of speech.

Those who advocated change were seen as troublemakers. Ted's father was appalled and worried that his son was openly expressing anti-establishment views. "You are not supposed to question the religious institutions. Don't question authority," his father told him.

"There were several people who were jailed or disappeared at the time because they were seen as a threat," explains Ted. "That was my parents' concern."

Ted was perhaps more willing to challenge authority than the rest of his family because of his age and his experiences in the world by that point. His parents and sisters had never attended school and his next brother was six years younger than he was. Ted had also spent the majority of his life since Grade 4 away from his family. "I learned how to cope by myself. That situation forced me to learn how to be an adult."

He ignored his father's advice and continued his criticisms of the government. He wouldn't have been able to live with himself had he kept quiet about the injustices happening around him.

Ted's outspoken behaviour in Grade 12 was not without costs. As a student leader, he had attended meetings to make decisions and express his and other students' opinions. He played a visible role as a spokesperson for the students, talking with city officials about various issues of concern. "Students were a huge political force at the time."

Ted was expelled from Grade 12 for a few days for editorials he wrote that questioned the monarchy. This drastic measure by the authorities did not sit well with Ted's schoolmates. "The students found out I was expelled and refused to go to classes until the school let me back in."

The high school had about 1,500 students at the time, and they all threatened to cause more problems for the police and community leaders if their demands were not met. The principal finally gave in and Ted was allowed to go back to school. But two conditions were imposed before he would be allowed through the doors again.

The students' union was dissolved and the newspaper was no longer allowed to print.

Schools and universities had been closed sporadically during the past several years of civil unrest. Sometimes the students closed them as a protest and other times, the government closed them to stop the 'breeding ground' of dissent in those institutions. The universities were closed in June 1973 when Ted finished Grade 12, and there was no indication of when they might re-open.

So Ted headed home to the farm to wait out the winter break and hope the university he wanted to attend in Addis Ababa would accept students again in September. If he couldn't start university, Ted couldn't be part of the national track team. His chance to fulfill his dreams of becoming a doctor and running in the Olympic Games would disappear.

* * *

What Ted thought would be several weeks at home turned into more than a year and a half of watching and waiting as the country's government continued to struggle.

Much of Ethiopia was in political turmoil in those years with teachers, taxi drivers, students, government workers and unemployed people holding sporadic demonstrations for better wages, improved education and an end to the famine. A mutiny of low-ranking military officers in early 1974 further weakened the emperor's authority[8] by ignoring and disobeying government directives.

Student agitators had heard rumblings about a group that was willing to overthrow the emperor and bring in the reforms that citizens were requesting. "We didn't even know who they were at the time. They were secretly formed," says Ted of the military officers who officially took power in June 1974. The Coordinating Committee of the Armed Forces, Police, and Territorial Army that came to be called the Derg (Amharic for 'committee')[9] was initially praised by the people.

"The Derg was sympathetic to our issues at first and we thought they supported us," says Ted. "We believed they would do as they said and be a provisional government bringing forward democratic elections. We thought we would have a voice to influence change and bring democratic reform. Of course, we were excited. We started expressing our opinion of how it should be."

Then things took a turn for the worse.

With Major Mengistu Haile Mariam as its chairman, the Derg took firm control of the government and started getting rid of any opposition.

In September 1974, Emperor Haile Selassie was arrested. He died under mysterious circumstances the following year. Some reports suggest he was suffocated in his sleep while other reports say he may have been strangled on orders from Mengistu.[10] Three days after the emperor was arrested, the Derg renamed itself the Provisional Military Administrative Council[11] and later added other groups to its government. It will forever be known as the Derg to those who lived under its rule, however.

Derg officers had little to no experience as leaders and were preoccupied with political disagreements with Eritrea and Tigre to the north while thousands of Ethiopians were dying of starvation due to drought. The Derg sought support from the Soviet Union, Cuba and other Warsaw pact countries and gave the U.S. presence in Ethiopia orders to leave. "In November 1974, the Derg brutally killed 68 former officials from Haile Selassie's government. They became a dictatorship themselves."

In December 1974, everyone who had a Grade 11 or higher education was ordered to be part of a literacy campaign called zemecha.[12] Students and teachers were ordered to go into the rural areas for two years to teach the citizens. Ted had no choice but to travel to a region near his home to become a teacher. While he embraced the goals of literacy, Ted was soon annoyed that instead of teaching reading and writing of the official Amharic language as he had expected, teachers were being asked to memorize Marxist-Leninist principles and instruct their students on that doctrine.

"The Derg members didn't want anyone to question their leadership. In their minds, they believed they were saviours," says Ted. "They were preaching quotes from Mao Tse-Tung, Vladimir Lenin and Joseph Stalin. We were encouraged to form study groups and study the Karl Marx doctrine. We didn't have any choice. The Communist Manifesto book was dumped free of charge everywhere. We were used to preach how good the military regime was and how people should be following the changes they were bringing for the country."

It was an assault on Ted's principles and, again, he rebelled.

"We were teaching things we didn't believe. We didn't want to be used as propaganda machinery."

After a few months, Ted and some other teachers left their postings to either go home or to Addis Ababa where they could hide from the military. They went from being called teachers to being labelled as traitors.

"We were classified as supporters of the opposition. We resisted attempts to be used and were called anti-revolutionaries and anarchists."

Ted does not regret his decision.

"The country was going through radical historical changes. Either you were with them or against them. There was nothing in between."

From early 1975 into early 1976, Ted spent most of his time at home but also visited friends in Addis Ababa and elsewhere. He stayed underground at the homes of different people who were sympathetic to the teachers' cause.

The Derg created groups of civilians called cadres who were loyal to the new regime.[13] These citizens were armed and were encouraged to agitate within communities. The Derg passed a law forbidding public gatherings and authorizing police and the cadre to shoot opponents of the government. Students and other intellectuals who did not support the governing Derg were at the top of the hit list.

"Rather than opposing them, we pretended to join them," Ted explains. When the cadres were meeting and talking about where their opponents might be hiding, friends who had infiltrated the cadres were able to warn students and teachers to move to another hiding spot before they were arrested or killed.

Prior to the creation of the Derg, Ted had participated in protest walks to oppose the government's policies and the appalling plight of starving Ethiopians. "When Haile Selassie was losing power, the military enjoyed the mass demonstrations and unrest. They used us to obtain power. When we started opposing the Derg, they didn't like it."

Ted was in Addis Ababa in March 1976 when he heard that a peaceful demonstration walk was being held from the university to the legislative buildings. He knew it was illegal to protest against the military regime, but his conscience demanded he join and support the walk. It was a decision that would change his life forever.

Several hundred university students, teachers and other educated workers started their walk calmly enough that day. They were not armed. It was just a peaceful demonstration of those expressing their dissatisfaction.

Ted walked near the front of the group chanting with others: 'Freedom of speech!' and 'We want elections!'

The protesters walked for 10 minutes when they turned a corner to discover that the military police had been notified of their protest. The police were blocking the road ahead and had no intention of allowing the protesters to continue their walk.

"All of a sudden, there was an army of trucks in front of us. Military officers carrying AK-47s jumped down from the back of the trucks and started randomly shooting."

The protesters were completely taken aback by this turn of events. They had never thought they'd be fired upon.

Ted had no time to think. He instinctively did what he does best.

He ran. For his life.

"There was panic and everybody was running different directions." Screaming people were pushing and falling all around him. Ted ran as fast as he could to get away from the guns. His mind was a blur of confusion and terror.

"I could feel some kind of sharp object hit me but I just kept running. After another five to 10 minutes of running, I began to feel some wetness in my shoe. When I looked down, I saw my pants were soaked in red. I didn't know I was shot until then. I passed out in shock."

Ted woke up the next morning in a police hospital, handcuffed and chained to the bed. He remained there for a couple of days, being treated for the wounds caused by a bullet which entered his left thigh on the inside and exited cleanly on the outside. Penny-sized scars still mark both spots. Ted is thankful for the doctors who patched him up in that hospital. The physical scars could have been much worse.

In the middle of his fourth night in hospital, military police threw Ted in the back seat of an army truck and started to drive. "I was worried I would be taken somewhere and shot," he remembers.

He couldn't see where they were taking him but later learned it was a converted military barracks in the highlands. The conditions were brutal. About 15 people were crammed into each cell – a closed-in room with only one highly-placed window for light and one locked door for entry and exit. Each detainee had a blanket and a few lucky ones had a small mattress to use on the cold concrete floor. There were no toilets and no running water inside.

* * *

Detention centre. Prison. Concentration camp. Ted has called it all these things, depending on the day and how fresh the wounds still feel to him.

Rarely has he spoken of his experiences there in all of the decades since. "No one would believe me," he says. Besides, the memories are still too painful.

Tears form in Ted's eyes as he thinks about his experiences in that building. He stops often to regain his composure when telling of the horrors he experienced there, but he has come to realize that talking about those experiences might actually help. Now that he is a respected athlete and community leader in his adopted country, more people might listen to him and learn from his past and it might help him to heal as well.

"You can never give up," he states with conviction. "You have to face the challenge that is before you and have faith in yourself that you will overcome. There's always hope."

Chapter Four

Bruised But Not Beaten

In times of war, horrific events occur which should not be repeated. However, some things must be told – to honour the victims, to express public outrage and to help discourage future wars.

The civil war in Ethiopia in the 1970s was similar to wars that have occurred in many other countries before and since. The group seizing power in Ethiopia attempted to crush its opposition. Citizens were harassed, apprehended, tortured, terrorized and traumatized. Some survived. Thousands did not.

Ted looks at his experiences in 1976 as ones that combined a bit of luck with a powerful determination to survive. He feels his young age of 21 gave him a better chance to come out alive. His strong desire to see his family again gave him hope.

Still, it's a miracle that he survived.

* * *

Shortly after arriving at the detention centre, Ted learned that many people had been killed in the protest and he was one of several survivors being held at this location with other prisoners.

"Most of the detainees were university students or high school teachers. Some were middle class citizens opposed to the Derg's policies. The government saw them all as a threat. If you didn't support them, you were a threat."

Crammed into a room "like sardines" with numerous other captives, Ted was forced to endure demoralizing conditions. There seemed to be a revolving door of detainees and some days, after the guards brought new people in, there were so many prisoners in the room that almost everyone had to stand. At times, people were lying on top of each other just to get a rest. It was almost impossible for the 6-foot-tall Ted to lie down comfortably, and he could never really relax.

Ted and the other prisoners did not know from one moment to the next what would happen to them. They thought they were going to be killed.

Lice and disease were common. Sanitation, non-existent. Twice a day, detainees were taken outside a few at a time to go to the toilet. Only twice a day, unless they were sick with dysentery.

They did their business in a putrid, disgusting outhouse under the stern eyes of the armed guards. They then walked over to a pipe that had running water coming from it to wash their hands. Many prisoners had stomach problems from drinking the unsanitary water. Disease spread quickly and everyone was filthy. Rarely were they allowed to take a bath or shower. It was a huge discomfort for a man like Ted who considered himself a neat freak in school.

The daily ration of food was a piece of bread in the morning and porridge at night, unless they were lucky enough to share a hot meal brought in by some family members of their fellow inmates. Since this was not an ordinary prison, family members of some of the detainees who lived in that region were allowed to come at night to bring hot food to their relatives. Parents were worried their children would soon be killed, so they brought them good meals of curried chicken, beef stew, or injera, which is a large circular pancake with cooked beans, meat or vegetables placed on it.

Ted's family did not know where he was, so he relied on the other detainees to share their hot food with him. Ted's usual fare was a biscuit and part of a thermos of tea or some porridge provided by the guards.

While in the hospital, the military police had interrogated Ted about the protest and its ringleaders. Ted was as honest as he could be without jeopardizing his own safety. He answered that there were no leaders. It was only a group of university students who wanted change. "We weren't organized. We just didn't want to be part of that regime."

The interrogations intensified in the detention centre.

They asked him what part of Ethiopia he came from. 'Why did you leave when you were assigned to teach?' That was, of course, another issue and he avoided answering that question.

Along with the interrogations came cruel punishment that Ted had never seen before and can barely talk about even to this day.

"Every evening, they took some of the detainees for interrogation. Some came back tortured. Some were injured and, because of the torture, were almost crippled. Some never came back."

While recalling the faces of his fellow prisoners and the pain they endured, Ted pauses in thought. He is still reluctant to talk about the most painful moments of his own life. He would rather focus on the positive things about Ethiopia, a land that he loved as a child and still loves today. These events occurred in the past and are, thankfully, over. But after many years of keeping the memories to himself, he has decided others might be able to learn a positive message about hope and overcoming adversity from these negative actions.

So he swallows hard, steels himself, and continues.

"We were sitting there worrying what would happen next. When we heard a knock on the door, we got so scared. Whose name would they call today? We knew some people never came back. It felt like we were waiting on death row. We were frightened like turtles, drawing into ourselves."

Each day, Ted waited in terror for his name to be called. It was called many times.

Detainees were taken to an interrogation room one at a time, surrounded by at least three guards who pointed guns at them. They were forced to sit on the cold concrete. The guards had poured cold water on the floor to make it even more uncomfortable. The prisoners were forced to clasp their hands together in front of their knees and were not allowed to speak until they were asked a question.

"They tied my wrists together in front of my knees and put a steel bar underneath my knees and on top of my arms to hold my arms back. Then they hung me upside down from the bar and hit the bottoms and sides of my feet."

As Ted remembers the torture, a loud sob escapes his mouth. He wipes away tears and after a moment, begins again.

"They were slapping, hitting and punching me everywhere. They hit me with sticks and chains and barbed wire from a fence. My feet were cut and bleeding. They were very swollen. Sometimes after they hit me, they made me walk on some blended rock and gravel on the floor. It was very painful. Or they hung me up and hit me again."

Each time, the brutality lasted several agonizing minutes.

Those who could not endure the pain sometimes signed whatever papers the guards gave them, including statements admitting they were involved in a conspiracy against the Derg. The prisoners didn't even know what would happen to them if they signed, but it looked like a better option than torture at the time.

Ted tried not to say too much when he was tortured. Some of the detainees gave the guards the names of people they knew had either died or fled the country. People who were safe from further punishment.

"There were times when I was interrogated that I didn't feel any pain at all," says Ted. "I blocked it out in my mind. Mentally, I was numb. Hours later or the next day, that's when I felt the pain."

Sometimes, he openly challenged his captors. "If you want to kill me, you can do it. You have the gun. There's nothing I can do," he told them.

He was punched and slapped, poked and prodded. A scar from a bayonet wound on his left abdomen is a permanent reminder of those episodes. "I thought at any time I could be killed but if I died, I knew I would be dying for a good cause."

There were many times when it was a struggle for Ted to hang on.

"When I was being tortured, at times I accepted I was going to die. I would lie down on the floor of my cell and dream about what it was going to be like in half an hour when I was dead. In those moments, I thought it would be better to expire than to prolong the suffering."

Ted would take himself away in his mind and dream of a calmer place where there was no pain. "I would dream about what heaven would be like. I was thinking about life after death. Ocean waves and blue skies. Sometimes in the dreams, I was floating. I was flying on wings. There were clouds. I felt I was going to a calmer place. It was very peaceful. It was a coping mechanism."

On days when Ted was stronger, he talked with other detainees he felt he could trust. They avoided talking about politics and spoke instead of the good days at home and in school, their grades and job ambitions. They talked about the importance of education. Some of the other detainees were intellectuals, fascinating people who went to schools in England and the U.S. Ted had never been out of the country. This new information and perspective were very interesting and it inspired him to consider leaving Ethiopia to get an education.

Some of the people in detention were individuals who had been bureaucrats in power before the Derg took control. Most of them were killed while in detention. Ted tries to mask his anger and frustration at this loss to his homeland, but he isn't entirely successful. "How many years will it take to produce educated people again? That unnecessary war was getting rid of their best people. They were either killed, jailed or left the country."

When Ted thinks back to how he felt when he was in the detention centre, he recalls many mixed emotions. "I was scared and angry and frustrated. I was not allowed to express how I felt. Inside, I was just melting. I was denying who I was. I had to lie to them about what I believed so I would not be killed. It was a horrible feeling."

It was the power of the human mind that kept Ted going. He was determined to do everything he could to live. "I decided to use my energy to survive. Things might be difficult but I would never give up."

Some of the detainees accepted offers from the military to stop the torture in exchange for becoming an informant in the cell. "They pretended they were tortured when they came back, but we knew. We were not stupid. They talked too much about how they opposed the government. They initiated discussions to get something out of us."

Others were asked by the guards to go back to their home regions and work for the government's goals. Ted rejected that idea, knowing if he did that, he would not be accepted in the community. Most of the population was against the Derg at that point.

Ted had no idea of what was happening in his village. He had not heard from his family for months before being imprisoned. He didn't have any clue if they knew where he was or even that he was alive. "I was also afraid to face my family. I knew my dad was going to be disappointed. I worried I was endangering their lives, too." Ted hoped that the government would not see his family as a threat related to the protest. They were, after all, uneducated peasants and had nothing to do with any of the unrest.

But he knew his family must be frightened. One of the Derg's tactics was to shoot an opponent and dump the dead body on the family's doorstep overnight. "In the morning, you could wake up and find your loved one's body."

It was an experience he hoped his family would never have to endure.

* * *

Six months after arriving at the detention centre, Ted and about 10 others were ushered out of the cell and into the dark night. The guards called their names and demanded the prisoners go with them. Ted thought the guards were taking him outside to shoot him.

There was not much moonlight and searchlights lit only portions of the courtyard. Ted and the others were told to sit on the ground, near the fence surrounding the barracks, with their hands on the back of their heads and their elbows touching their knees. He heard a truck arrive at the gate, likely bringing in new detainees. Then there was a huge commotion of yelling and noise, followed by gunfire.

Ted thought someone must have been trying to escape or resist arrest. There was a lot of confusion and when he glanced up, he saw that the guard with an AK-47 rifle who had been watching over him and the other prisoners was no longer standing there. Ted quickly decided to grab this slim chance of hope and try to escape.

He ran over to a pile of lumber lying on the ground near the fence and quickly jumped on top of it. He hoisted himself up over the top of the concrete fence and barely noticed that the top of the concrete was imbedded with broken glass. He fell about three metres down to the ground on the other side.

Then he stood up and ran for his life once more.

"It was dark. They couldn't see me. I ran. I was barefoot. I ran and ran."

Ted didn't stop running and didn't look back until he had gone at least 20 kilometres. He was vaguely familiar with the area, having walked some of these paths to visit friends who lived there when he was younger. But walking during the day was different than running for one's life at night.

"I was not running like you run a race. I was running away from death."

Ted often tripped and fell on the ground because of the darkness.

He eventually climbed an evergreen tree near a farmer's field to get away from the noisy hyenas and to rest for a while. When he stopped, he was exhausted and confused. Then he remembered something else. His feet.

"When I was running for my life, I didn't think about the pain at all. When I stopped running, that's when I felt it. I sat and wondered: 'How did I run with this agony?' "

Running on cut and swollen feet seems like more than a human being could bear, but Ted had done it. "How powerful our mind is to be able to block that. There is more strength within us than we know."

Ted tried to relax but he couldn't do so for long. "I tried to have a nap in the tree but, in my mind, I kept seeing the soldiers chasing me. In the detention centre, the gun was always pointed at us. I could still imagine the guards, with their guns pointing at me. I knew if I got caught, I would be dead."

Shortly before sunrise, Ted was running again.

In the daytime, he hid in straw piled high in farmers' fields. During the night, he ran even further away from the detention centre. He did this for two days, having time to reflect on what had happened only when he rested.

He had made a sudden decision and acted on it. And it saved his life.

"I made a split-second choice to conquer that environment. I had to use that moment. The chaos was my window of opportunity and I knew that was the right time to go."

Sitting there on the ground, Ted had appeared to be following orders, but his oppressors had no way of knowing what was going on in his mind. He later heard that most of those detainees were transferred to a regular prison with real criminals – without being charged. Many of the detainees did not go to court for many years.

By the third night, Ted was completely exhausted and totally confused. He had not eaten for three days and was weak with hunger and thirst. In the evening, he ventured out on to a farmer's field and started eating raw grain that had fallen from the plants. A horse was grazing nearby and his presence startled it, alerting the farmer that there was someone or something in his field.

Ted couldn't see the farmer and thought he was safe. When the farmer called out, Ted panicked and started running again. The farmer called to Ted to stop.

"He yelled: 'Son, don't run. I'll help you. What's your name?' I was confused and weak and I started to cry."

The farmer gave Ted some food and secretly nursed him back to health over the next week. During that time, the farmer heard news about the detention centre riot and told Ted that a few other people had escaped the barracks that night as well. Ted's heart soared, but only temporarily. He was still, after all, a political dissident and a wanted man sleeping in straw piles at night and being looked after by a farmer he did not know but had to trust.

Fortunately, the farmer's family was away from home then, and the farmer was the only one who knew of this escaped prisoner lying in his field. Ted was grateful the farmer was sympathetic to what the students and intellectuals were doing for the country.

The farmer gave Ted a pair of military boots to wear but the next day, they realized that it was not wise to wear the boots because the military was feared. Ted also didn't want people to notice anything unusual about his footwear, so the farmer gave him a pair of sandals made locally from tires. Most of the farmers wore this type of sandal, and Ted had a better chance of going unnoticed with this footwear. "A farmer's foot is very rough, with callouses, and my feet at the time looked similar to that. Some of my toenails were lost from the consistent hitting in the detention centre, and my feet were very swollen."

After Ted recuperated somewhat, the farmer proposed two plans. He suggested Ted could either go live with the farmer's relatives on the Nile River delta or take a bus and then walk to where Ted's own family lived. Ted went back to the pile of straw he had been hiding in and mulled over his options, realizing he didn't really feel good about either idea.

In the past, Ted had often relied on his intuition to make decisions on where to go and what to do. "There are times when I know that what I desire is not what is right for me. I use intuition to guide me." His instincts did not fail him this time, either.

The farmer came back later that day and informed Ted that the bus station was no longer safe. Many people had been arrested there and Ted was sure to get caught if he attempted to go home that way. The farmer then asked another man to take Ted to the Nile delta.

"That man said he would go to the store first to get supplies and then come get me. Something in my gut said this did not feel right. So I just left the farmer's field and started walking towards my family's village."

Ted avoided the cities and the major roads, keeping to the smaller paths and away from curious eyes. He walked mostly at night and hid in farmers' fields, bushes or up in trees during the day. He knew it was best to sleep close to a village to avoid the wild animals, but not close enough to be seen.

It was October and the fields were full of corn and peas, so that's what Ted ate. It took him more than four days of walking to reach his parents' home. He arrived late one night and was greeted with a combination of surprise, confusion, joy and fear.

"They knew what had happened. They knew I had escaped, but they were scared. They could get in trouble for giving me shelter. My mom hugged me and was crying. My dad couldn't believe I was alive."

Ted stayed in the region for much of the next two years. He hid in nearby caves or bushes in the hills during the warmer weather and stayed in different homes in the village when it was colder outside.

One of the people who brought Ted food while he was in the hills was his teenage sister, Sadate. As a female and the youngest of Ted's siblings, she was beyond suspicion. With the help of some of Ted's other family members, young Sadate packed a few day's worth of non-perishable food supplies for Ted and the other four men who eventually joined him in hiding. Sadate pretended she was going to collect firewood and walked up the narrow mountain path that only a few of them knew about. She left food at a pre-arranged spot.

If the men changed their hiding spot in the hills, one of them went into the village the night before and left a message about where they wanted Sadate to bring the next batch of supplies. In between these trips, Ted and his friends ate whatever they could find in the hills, including the fruit from fig trees and honey from beehives. They hunted and occasionally killed a wild bird. They drank their fill of water from ponds or the crystal clear mountain streams in the area.

The dry food would last for a few days but they rarely had enough to fill their stomachs. "We were often hungry and always tired. When you're in hiding, you don't sleep and you are always alert, on edge. We had watchtowers in the rocks on the hills. We hid behind and between the rocks where we could see if anyone was coming up the path. We were always watching that narrow path. There was only enough room for people to travel one direction."

It was a stressful existence made a little easier because of the monkeys who lived on the hills around them.

Each monkey troop has its own guard that stands watch so other animals don't sneak up on them. The guard chattered loudly when it saw anything out of the ordinary, so the men knew when someone was coming up the path. The monkeys had grown used to the men hiding on the hills among them, and only reacted when other humans or a predator such as a cheetah came along.

While in hiding, Ted constantly worried about jeopardizing the safety of his family and friends, so he rarely told anyone the truth about his plans or where he was going to stay when he came into the village on cold nights. He tried to blend in by dressing like a local farmer and went into hiding again any time he heard from a merchant or someone else that militia or security personnel were thought to be in the area.

When he was in the village, Ted often saw children running carefree on the hills near his home, but he didn't allow himself to give much thought to his own lost running career.

He could only think about surviving.

* * *

At this point, Ted was still convinced that things might change and democracy was still a possibility for Ethiopia. He was hopeful that the government would fall or would change its policies because of the opposition.

That, of course, did not happen.

In November 1977, Mengistu Haile Mariam took even more control of the Derg and eliminated most of his opponents during the next few years. Mengistu stepped up the Derg's campaign of 'Red Terror,' named after the Communist campaign of mass arrests and deportations during the Russian Civil War. From 1975 to 1978, tens of thousands of people were imprisoned, terrorized or killed during the official period of the Ethiopian Red Terror.[14]

Shortwave radios were common across Ethiopia by then and the Derg used the airwaves to extend its reach through the countryside. In the hills, Ted listened to the radio to keep track of the current political situation and was often horrified by what he heard.

"Every night on the news, they started the military marching music and they announced the names of those who had been killed that day for opposing the regime. It was frightening. When I heard that military marching song start, I felt terror. I would look around and could feel their presence. It was a method of fear-mongering to scare people and conquer."

In 1977, the Derg introduced an amnesty as a response to increased resistance from the public. They had been pressured, particularly by parents, who cried out that their children were disappearing.

"I didn't trust that it was a genuine offer and I did not accept it," recalls Ted. "Some of the dissidents did accept amnesty and went back.

Some accepted government positions in the area and they didn't get a good reception from the community. Some of our friends surrendered and most of them were killed afterwards. I was still in hiding."

In March 1978, Ted learned from a travelling merchant and from a friend who had infiltrated the cadre that the militia was on its way to arrest them. This type of warning had come before.

Some militia members were not interested in fighting but had been conscripted to take up arms. On previous occasions, these members had sent messages prior to the militia's arrival warning the residents when they were expected to get to the village. 'Advise your children to leave the area,' the message said.

When this latest warning came, Ted and his friends grabbed a few more non-perishable supplies and headed further up into the hills to a plateau near a fresh clean pond at the forest's edge. They thought they could survive there for several months without being caught. That had been their thinking, until one of the men didn't return to the camp one night.

They had run out of food and had asked the man to trap a wild bird at sunset near the water. The others waited at their hiding place in anticipation of a good meal. "It was not fun. It was survival," says Ted. The man did not come back with food and Ted and his friends panicked, wondering what had happened.

They left their hiding spot and called out his name. He did not answer and finally, Ted found his footsteps leading down from the narrow path and into the village. Ted went into the village to the home of the man's parents to find out if they knew where he was.

The man had decided he could no longer bear the stress of continual hiding. He planned to surrender to the militia and accept the amnesty. His parents urged Ted and the others to do the same.

The militia was about a day away from the village and they had to make a decision.

They knew they couldn't stay in their hiding place because the man would likely lead the militia right to them. There was no other acceptable option. Ted knew that this meant the end of his time with his family. He had to leave Ethiopia.

"That evening, I went to Sadate and quickly said goodbye. I didn't talk to anyone else in my family. There was no time. I hugged Sadate and told her we might not see each other again. I might be killed."

He and the others took only a few dry goods and essential items that they could easily carry. Their knapsacks held a couple simple khaki shirts, a single pair of underwear, a peasant-style pair of shorts, one pair of denim jeans and locally-made sandals. They left the village and started walking west towards Sudan.

They had small bags of salted roasted grain to eat and stopped to drink from the ponds and streams along the way whenever they got thirsty, but it was impossible to nourish their souls. Their hearts were breaking with each step they took farther away from home.

They later heard that the man had indeed led the militia to their hiding spot. Fortunately, they were no longer there. The man was arrested and put in prison, where he died later that same year.

Ted also learned that his family and friends in the village suffered considerably after his escape. When the militia got to the village, they made Ted's family watch as they burned their home and grain bins to the ground. Other homes belonging to those suspected of sheltering the escaped men were also burned. Some villagers were brutally beaten, raped or tortured.

"My mom was arrested for six months. My dad was not arrested at the time because he was with the livestock in a remote area. My younger siblings were under house arrest but allowed to go to school."

When the family returned to the village after their detention, their lives had changed. They were now considered anti-government activists and were harassed for several years after that by government militia. Ted is still upset that his family suffered because of him. Other people in the village blamed his parents for the damage to their homes. Ted's parents moved to a different area to build a new home and new lives.

For most of his adult life, Ted has blamed himself for the attack on his family.

When he thinks about a response to the question of whether it was really his fault, Ted leans forward with his head in his hands and emits a heart-wrenching sob. He still hurts for his family, friends and himself but knows he is not entirely to blame for the pain they suffered.

Yes, he was a vocal opponent of the government and yes, his family felt obligated to feed and hide him after he escaped from the detention centre. But he was not the only one caught in this situation. His was not the only family hurt during those days.

"It happened throughout Ethiopia. It was beyond our control. It's the guilt we have lived through," he says of the survivors.

"The government saw us as a threat. You could not be neutral in those times. I never dreamed of leaving my country. At the time, I thought: 'The government will fall. It will get better.'"

But the government continued its reign of terror and Ted had no choice. He had to flee his homeland.

"We faced a dark future at the time. We didn't know what would happen to us, but we escaped death."

Chapter Five

Desperation

After leaving their homes, Ted and the other men walked for four nights on narrow paths down the hills and through the tall grasses of Ethiopia's lowlands toward the Sudan border. They were careful not to speak while they walked. They listened intently and if they heard people talking, they jumped off the path and into the bushes, where they waited until the others had passed.

The trip was long and arduous. When they arrived at a town on the border, they were filled with fear and anguish, having no idea what was ahead. There was also considerable sadness, knowing they might never be able to return to Ethiopia after that night.

Ted was sweating, and it wasn't just from the heat. He was scared. What if they were caught? What if they were sent back to prison and tortured again? He'd rather die. And maybe he would.

There was still a long way to go before he tasted freedom, and he wouldn't allow himself to think too long about the horrible possibilities. He was determined to get out of the country alive.

"I was raised to not give up and to be resilient. If I got caught, I knew I would be facing life in prison, or death."

Ted and his friends hired a guide to help them get across the border. Together, they hid in some bushes just outside the town and watched the events at the crossing until they could formulate a plan for getting into Sudan undetected. They noticed that the border guards were focusing attention on the outside edges of the town where smugglers took people illegally over the border. The guards did not look like they expected anyone to come through the middle of the town.

So Ted and his friends decided their best opportunity to cross would be at three o'clock in the morning when there would be fewer guards and less chance of getting caught. They chose to take the less-expected method of sneaking through the town instead of going through the wide-open areas near the border crossing. They hoped they were making the right decision.

"We were very nervous but the majority decided we had to take that route through town," explains Ted. "We studied the situation very well and we took a risk."

The men snuck quickly through the village, careful not to get too close to any homes with dogs that might alert the guards of their presence. Once they got through town, they ran as fast as they could across the border and kept on running until they were tired.

Still functioning on adrenaline, Ted knew he was now safely out of Ethiopia and into a new country. The moment he stopped running, however, his world temporarily fell apart.

"Everything caved in. I realized that I didn't have a home or a country any more. This was not my country and I could not go back. It was a devastating moment."

The terror he felt in Ethiopia was suddenly replaced with an overwhelming fear of the unknown.

"When you're forced out of your country, there is no normal life. You become homeless. You've lost everything, including your pride."

Ted was worried he still might be stopped in Sudan and deported back to Ethiopia. The only choice open to him and the others was to continue on and hope for the best. So they kept walking, heading for the nearest Sudanese town.

The terrain changed quite dramatically from bamboo trees and tall grasses in Ethiopia to a semi-arid desert in Sudan. The temperature was at least 35 degrees Celsius under the cloudless sky and the men were exhausted both physically and emotionally.

When they reached the next town, they went to the local school for assistance. Sudan is a Muslim country and Ted and his friends didn't understand the culture or the language. They could only hope that the Sudanese teachers spoke English so they could converse somewhat. The Ethiopians all spoke broken English, having taken it as a subject in high school. They were pleased to see that the Sudanese teachers also knew some English and could talk with them.

The teachers fed the men a simple meal under the shade of a tree, then took them to the local police station, where the men were detained for a week to determine whether they were legitimate refugees.

"The police interviewed us about why we left Ethiopia. At the time, Emperor Haile Selassie's supporters in Sudan were trying to recruit young people to go back and fight. We told them we were not here for that reason."

Ted and his friends had to stay on the grounds. At night, they slept on a mattress in the back courtyard. They were not locked up because they were not prisoners. They were just low-level houseguests who were kept on the grounds of the jailhouse because it was cheaper than putting them in a hotel.

The police finally decided the men were legitimate refugees and escorted them by train to the Ministry of Immigration office in Khartoum, Sudan's capital city. There, they were interviewed again and given a letter that stated they were eligible for refugee status and financial assistance from the United Nations High Commission for Refugees. The letter was a sign of hope, but there were no guarantees and the line-up for help turned out to be long.

"When we got to the United Nations office, we saw that there were several hundred people displaced. Most of the refugees were there because of the war in Eritrea. We saw it could take days or weeks to be called forward for assistance. Sometimes we lined up all day and didn't get to the front. We had to go back the next day."

Ted and the others had no money, food or shelter. They begged for food and money from the Sudanese people and found shelter at the Ethiopian Orthodox Church, where the priest offered them a spot to sleep behind the church in the large fenced outdoor courtyard. There, the refugees were each given a bed sheet and warned to take care of their possessions.

Conditions were usually very sparse and often frightening. The crime rate was high among the many refugees waiting for relief. People stole from others who had better clothes than they did. Ted's jeans were stolen on one occasion. He had washed them and hung them up to dry at night. In the morning, they were gone. The priest wasn't surprised by the theft. He had warned the men it could happen. Fortunately, he was a kind-hearted man and gave Ted a new pair of pants.

Ted recalls another time when a friend of his went to the local park to nap under the trees in an attempt to escape the 40-degree heat. His money was stolen from his back pocket while he rested. "People watched you and took advantage of you in your weak moments, stealing either your money or belongings. It never happened to me. When I was napping, I made sure I kept my money and everything I had in my front pocket."

Ted isn't sure he could have slept if he wanted to. His sleeping patterns had been significantly altered in his homeland. When he was hiding in the hills, a small noise would wake him up. "I never had a peaceful sleep during my last years in Ethiopia."

After only two weeks of lining up in Khartoum, Ted and his friends were pleasantly surprised to have made it to the front of the United Nations line. They received less than $20 CDN each as a temporary amount to help them survive. The refugees could go back for additional money occasionally if they could get through the lines, which were growing as the wars in neighbouring countries increased the flow of refugees to Sudan.

Ted and his friends quickly figured out how to work with others to improve their own situation. They developed a sharing mechanism with other refugees and some humanitarian organizations, and learned how to ask for more help.

The Blue Nile River originates in Ethiopia, flowing southeast from Lake Tana and cutting through some of the world's largest gorges, that are longer and wider than North America's Grand Canyon.[15] In Khartoum, the Blue Nile joins the Nile River, known by locals as the White Nile. Some days, Ted woke early and walked a half hour from the church courtyard to the Nile River to bathe or have a refreshing swim before lining up at the U.N. office for extra assistance. Sometimes he took soap to wash with but not every morning, because soap was in short supply and it also contaminated the river. The refugees also swam in the Nile in the middle of the day to cool down.

After a month of sleeping in the church courtyard, Ted and his friends were told they had to take their assistance money and leave. They found a one-room shack in a ghetto area on the outskirts of Khartoum where most of the refugees were barely surviving.

They purchased mattresses for each of them, so no one had to sleep on the dirt floor, and a small kerosene stove to cook their meals. They had to be careful with their money.

Ted spent most of his days in the public library trying to figure out what to do next. Although he read and researched possible ways out of his situation, it was sometimes hard to stay awake in the comfort of the air-conditioned building, which was preferable to the heat of the day and the tiny shack he now called home. Ted had not been sleeping properly because of the warm temperatures, his own physical malnourishment and emotional and physical exhaustion. He could stay in the library if he was reading. If he fell asleep, he was kicked out. Ted was asked to leave on several occasions.

While in Khartoum, Ted's curiousity, ingenuity and open-minded nature helped him to learn about this new culture and blend in as best he could. "Sudan is mostly Muslim. As a Christian, it was a new experience for me. When the people asked my name, I would tell them it was Mohammed. I did this to fit in. It made my life easier. I also walked into the mosque and prayed with them. I respect their beliefs in Allah. They even invited me home and fed me."

Ted remembers a young Sudanese man, educated in England, who invited Ted to his home for supper. Ted was surprised to see that the man's wife and children did not join them for the meal. In the Muslim tradition, women serve the meal to the men and then eat in the kitchen with the children. It was a culture shock for Ted to see this type of mealtime practice. In Ethiopia, the whole family eats together and children even have priority at times, being fed before the adults have their meals.

Overall, Ted enjoyed his time with the Sudanese people. "They are very generous. It was fascinating to have an opportunity to learn about their culture."

Ted's adaptability has helped him overcome many obstacles over the years. The challenges he faced when he was younger taught him patience, tolerance and the ability to get comfortable in almost any situation.

"It is human nature to judge others with a first impression. I try not to do that."

* * *

By June 1978, the wars in Eritrea and Ethiopia had forced thousands more refugees into Khartoum, and the Sudanese government was under pressure to ease the situation. "We were a nuisance for the people of Sudan. They had their own unemployment problems without us creating more strain on their economy."

Ted and his friends were told that if they wanted any further assistance from the United Nations, they had to go live in a refugee camp away from Khartoum. Some of his friends chose not to make the journey but Ted decided the camp might provide him with more opportunities for a better life. Getting there meant taking a long bus ride on a paved road used to carry goods in from the Red Sea.

The refugee camp was typical of those on modern-day news reports, consisting of row after row of makeshift tents and shacks with dirt floors and unsanitary, shared open latrines dug in the ground in a common area. There was very little to eat and often contaminated water supplies. His living conditions did not improve at all from what he had faced in the ghetto. There was little hope for the future.

"It was very rough. About five of us lived in a small shack with a dirt floor. There was no running water, no electricity, no toilets. It was crowded and unsanitary. People were sick all the time. We survived on handouts. That was humiliating."

Shortly after arriving at the camp, Ted saw a posting for an auto mechanic course funded by the United Nations. He and about 10 others were accepted into the classes. Even though the course was only two months long, Ted was ecstatic to be allowed in.

He and the other students did not consider the auto mechanic course as a career that would help them much in the future, but it did give them an opportunity to get short-term help. They received a small amount of spending money that they used to rent a small apartment for five people, and they could temporarily feed themselves. When the course was over, they had to go back to the camp.

Ted did not use the auto mechanic skills he learned for many years. He had never been mechanically inclined and his family did not own a vehicle, so it was all new information that he had no opportunity to utilize. While he learned things about fan belts and how to change engine oil or tires, automobile knowledge was wasted on him until years later when he purchased his own vehicle.

The refugee camp in Sudan was the worst in living conditions that brought out the worst in human behaviour. People were starving and desperate, unwilling to share because of the scarcity of food.

That type of conduct was against Ted's upbringing and it hurt him to watch others treat fellow human beings that way. "My mom used to say: 'If you do a good thing, a good thing will happen to you.' She taught me not to be selfish."

Ted's time in the refugee camp was one of the lowest points in his life. There was no reason to get up in the morning and no change in the routine. "The days were long. One week felt like one year. It was scorching hot and I lacked even the most basic things. I worried that if I had breakfast, there was no guarantee I would also have lunch. There were a few times when I contemplated suicide to get out of that misery. I longed for a normal life."

Ted started smoking, paying a few cents for a bundle of cornhusks that he used to roll up the tobacco he purchased locally. It was a crutch at the time to help him cope with emotional distress.

He also finally gave up on the idea of ever returning to Ethiopia. The Mengistu government had an even stronger hold on the country, so Ted decided to focus instead on what his future might look like away from his homeland. He tried to be optimistic.

He said to himself: "I cannot give up hope. Anything will be better than this and it will improve."

Ted wondered how he could get out of the mess he was in. He knew that he alone held the answers to his future. "The solution is me. I knew I needed to work hard to make things better, and I was ready to explore any opportunity I could find. I decided I would not use the excuse of what happened in the past to hold me back. I would ignore it. I reminded myself that the past was gone. Tomorrow will be different."

As he has continued to do for most of his adult life, Ted turned away from the negatives and surrounded himself with people in the camp who would, like him, focus on improving their lives. He tried to select friends who had the same positive attitude. It helped him survive.

As a coping mechanism, he often thought back to his successful running days in Ethiopia. "It was one way to distract me from the agony of my present situation. I came across a running magazine that featured high-achieving athletes. I would dream and visualize myself running, winning and being recognized on the podium. A fellow refugee saw me dreaming and affirmed that my dream might some day become a reality. He gave me the belief that I could be a success. It gave me hope."

Meanwhile, Ted kept trying to find any type of work or training opportunity that he could. He was not successful.

After nine dismal months in Sudan, he and some others decided to leave for a chance at a better life elsewhere.

CHAPTER SIX

LIGHT AT THE END OF THE TUNNEL

In December 1978, Kenya seemed to beckon Ted with more opportunities for education and a better life, if only temporarily. The country had more aid agencies within its boundaries than Sudan and Ted hoped to tap into some of those resources and perhaps even find a way out of Africa. He knew it would be difficult to get into Kenya but felt it was worth a try.

He and five other young men decided to go to Kenya through southern Sudan and Uganda. The only way they could get there was by steamship on the Nile River. The steamer was slow as a snail going against the current and they spent about eight days on the river.

Those who had enough money purchased a room with a bed. Others like Ted, who could only afford the minimum fee, sat on their blankets in whatever open space they could find on the flatbed deck. They ate non-perishable food they each carried with them and drank water provided by the steamer company.

During the trip, the passengers on deck could only get up, walk around a bit and then go back to their spots and sleep. Ted enjoyed seeing crocodiles, hippopotamuses and jumping fish in the water. He also watched for snakes and crocodiles on the shore as the boat slowly made its way up the Nile.

The steamer dropped the men off at Juba in southern Sudan. Ted and the others then had to bribe officials to let them into Uganda. This was during Idi Amin's rule and Uganda was in anarchy, which played to Ted's advantage. Bribery was to become a big part of his existence over the next few years.

To leave Uganda, he hitched a ride with a sympathetic delivery truck driver who came from Ethiopia. It was Christmas Eve and when the border patrol officers approached the truck, the driver wished them Merry Christmas and pressed money into their hands. The officers then didn't ask to see Ted's papers. When they arrived at the Kenya border, those officials asked who Ted was but were more than happy to let him pass once the driver introduced him as his helper and gave the officials a little bit of money.

"Corruption was everywhere. If you had money, you could go anywhere. We didn't have a lot of money, but enough to get through."

Ted considered himself lucky to have survived to this point and once again, luck played a factor in this part of his journey. "The truck driver was from Ethiopia and we spoke the same language. He said to me: 'My son's about your age. You could be my son and this could happen to him. I can help you.' In Nairobi, he dropped me off where most of the Ethiopian refugees lived and said: 'Son, good luck.' And he was gone."

Ted spent his first few nights in Nairobi staying with some Ethiopian refugees he met there. The terrain in Nairobi was more similar to Ted's homeland than was Sudan. The city is about 1660 metres (5450 feet) above sea level, slightly higher than his home village, and the temperature peaks at around 25 degrees Celsius. Nairobi is close to the Great Rift Valley with Mount Kilimanjaro to the southeast,[16] and is more multicultural than Sudan, which made Ted's adjustment there easier.

When he applied for asylum in Kenya, Ted didn't want the immigration officers to know he had come via Sudan because he feared they wouldn't accept him after Sudan had given him temporary asylum. So when they asked where he was from, Ted responded, "Ethiopia."

He was relieved when, after a week, he was given a permit granting him temporary asylum in Kenya. This gift was not without cost, though, as he had to re-apply to immigration authorities every three months to renew that permit. This added more stress to an already-tense situation.

The United Nations refugee commission's system in Kenya was, thankfully, a different system than the one in place in Sudan. It was more structured. There were still desperate people lined up all the time and they were all needy, but it was manageable.

The United Nations gave Ted and every other refugee 150 Kenyan shillings each month (about $20 CDN then). This was a significant improvement from Sudan because he could now rely on funds coming to him on a regular basis. His decision to leave Sudan was already paying off.

That gift of money wasn't the end of his troubles, though. It still wasn't much, and the only area he could afford to live in was in a slum area on the outskirts of Nairobi. He and some others rented a small one-room house with a dirt floor and metal roof. They had to get water from a pipe outside the building.

Although not technically a refugee camp, the conditions in this ghetto area were similar. "When you are in exile, it's not a picnic or a holiday," explains Ted. "You are very vulnerable. Conditions were terrible. We lived in a shantytown. I had to be strong and believe that I could overcome that adversity as well."

Refugees were not allowed to look for work, so Ted spent most of his time in his first weeks there searching for education and immigration opportunities. He applied for scholarships through the United Nations but he was not successful. Then he got lucky with an application for a graphic design scholarship through a German humanitarian organization.

The Otto Benecke Stiftung Foundation, named after a student movement leader in Germany, helps evacuees and refugees work towards employment. Dozens of applicants, including Ted, had an oral interview to compete for only two scholarships. Several days later, a representative of the foundation met with all the applicants at once to make her announcement. Ted waited nervously to hear what came next.

"She said: 'I'm going to be announcing only two names. I am sorry I can't offer it to all of you.' The first name she called was mine. I was just speechless. I could not believe it. I started crying. I was full of joy."

The three-year scholarship to Kenya Polytechnic improved Ted's lifestyle dramatically. Instead of the 150 Kenyan shillings he received from the United Nations every month, the scholarship gave him 1,000 shillings a month. Scholarship winners could stay at a hostel instead of in the dirty slum area and be fed nutritious regular meals there. The scholarship also gave them an increased chance of work after graduation.

From the middle of 1979 to spring 1982, Ted went to school and life was sort of normal. He was in a co-operative program that mixed schooling for six months with work experience at the local newspaper for the next six months.

Some students used their extra money to take an illegal plane ride to Europe, travelling to Italy or Germany in the hopes of eventually attaining refugee status, but Ted had heard those students had to stay underground for several years before being accepted as legitimate refugees in those countries. It was not what he wanted to do with his life.

While he took full advantage of the schooling and work experiences, he couldn't bear to keep his good fortune to himself. He shared his money with some of his friends who had not received that scholarship opportunity. Some people told him he was naïve. They advised him to save it for himself, but Ted couldn't do it. "Everybody was desperate. Everyone was starving and getting sick. It didn't feel right to just watch them and keep that money in my pocket."

After two months in the hostel, he paid for a better place away from the slum. There was a sink inside the room and a shared shower and washroom in the hallway. They had small cupboards for their food but still had to buy fresh food every day. There was no refrigerator of course, and if they wanted milk, they had to buy a small container and use it right away or share the remainder with others before the milk went sour.

This new one-room apartment would be considered tiny and sparse by North American standards, but it was a mansion to Ted at the time. "There was electricity. We had one big mattress for a couple of people and we took turns sleeping on the floor. It was like going from hell to heaven."

With Ted's extra scholarship money, he and his friends were finally able to fill their stomachs every day. "For the first time since I left Ethiopia, I was not starving anymore and I could feed others. We didn't have to worry."

* * *

Wars and difficult times bring people together who, in a calmer world, would have been unlikely friends. Some of the men that Ted roomed with in Sudan and Kenya, for example, later immigrated to the United States. He has rarely seen them since.

Wars can also cause otherwise sane-thinking people to sometimes make illogical, life-limiting decisions.

In Kenya, one of Ted's high school classmates was unable to bear the problems they were facing. He went back to Ethiopia through the repatriation program with the U.N. and went to school and university there. Before he left Kenya, Ted had asked the man for his mattress to give to someone else who needed one. The man asked Ted if he was stupid and wondered why Ted would let others take advantage of him. "No, you have to pay me," he told Ted. "But I know if it was you, you would give it to me for free."

Ted couldn't understand his friend's reluctance to give away the mattress, as he would have done. It wasn't that he didn't know how to take advantage of others. He simply didn't want to do it. It was not in his nature.

Years later, Ted learned that when a new government gained control of Ethiopia, his friend was arrested and jailed. The man died in an Ethiopian prison.

Ted occasionally wonders what might have happened to his friend if he had stayed in Kenya. Would he still be alive today?

* * *

Although Ted was pleased with the schooling and better living conditions in Kenya, his daily interactions with the Kenyan authorities were stressful. He often had to bribe the immigration officers to renew his permit, using the corrupt system to his advantage to stay in the country at that time.

Refugees who had money could buy any document they wanted, including travel papers issued by the United Nations. Ted avoided those temptations and concentrated on his education and figuring out a way to leave the country legally. However, he was still traumatized by any authority figure and his regular run-ins with the local police left him fearful.

"Several times the Kenyan police arrested us for no reason except for a bribe. If we gave them whatever we had, even $1, they left us alone."

On one occasion, Ted and some others went to have a beer to celebrate with a friend who had been accepted as an immigrant to the United States. The police stormed in and asked them for money. When they couldn't come up with enough money to make the police happy, the men were accused of being illegal aliens and put in jail.

The interior of that jail was among the worst places Ted had ever been in. Each cell had several people in it and there was barely enough room to sit or lie down. "The washroom was broken. Human waste was everywhere."

Ted also remembers his disgust at being locked up with drunks, thieves and criminals. "Being locked up with these convicts was worse than when I was in detention in Ethiopia. The people in Ethiopia were not dangerous drunks or drug addicts. They were intellectuals and very fascinating people."

The men spent the next few days there in fear of their surroundings and worrying that their friend might miss his flight to the U.S. Finally, a United Nations worker from Austria visited the Kenyan jail and helped them. He reluctantly paid a bribe to the police, and Ted and his friends were released.

The U.N. worker's fiancée was visiting Kenya at the time and he purposely took her to the jail to see the inhumane conditions there. "I could see on her face that she could not believe what she was seeing. One of our friends brought us food and we were starving, grabbing food as fast as we could. The U.N. worker said to us after: 'I wanted her to see this to appreciate what she has at home.' That man saved us. He knew how to deal with the authorities and he was there to help us."

Occasionally when Ted was in Kenya, he would briefly think about his lost running career. He was, after all, in the country that was home to some of the greatest distance runners in the world. Sometimes, he walked to the Nairobi track to watch the Kenyan Olympic running team while they trained.

"This is the sport I cherish," he explains. It was free, satisfying entertainment to watch the runners. While he was sad at not being able to to run himself, it wasn't his priority at that time. "Survival was my number one priority. Running was a privilege. It was not a necessity. I had to find a country to live in."

At the beginning of Ted's final year of his graphic design scholarship, he was becoming increasingly anxious to have a plan in place on how to leave Kenya. He realized that when he finished school, the scholarship money would be done and there would be no guarantees of further financial help. "I would have new skills but no certainty of a job. I might be living a desperate life again."

The country was also becoming more crowded with refugees from Uganda and elsewhere. "The Kenyan people were sick of us. I don't blame them. We were a nuisance to them."

The constant harassment by police and the perpetual need to bribe immigration officials to get his permit renewed were also taking a toll. "I never had any problems with the people of Kenya. It was the law enforcement officers. They took advantage of the most vulnerable people.

It's disgraceful for people in a power position to use their power for financial gain."

When he was looking for a country to move to, Ted did not consider anywhere in Europe because he heard it was becoming too crowded there. He applied to Canada, the United States and Australia, but grew restless waiting for a response.

Every day, he would go to the mailbox in hopes of good news from an immigration office. When he got a letter, he was scared to read what was inside.

Canada's 1981 Census of its citizens showed that only 2.7% of the 16% of immigrants in Canada that year were of African descent.[17] The borders weren't opening up too quickly for African immigrants at the time Ted wanted to move to Canada, but that didn't stop him from thinking about the possibility.

Canada's reputation was very positive, known as a country that supported multiculturalism. Canada was also being lobbied by the United Nations to open its borders further to African refugees. Ted hoped he would be one of the few Africans that Canada let through its doors.

His optimism paid off. He received a message to go to the Canadian embassy for an interview. After he completed that step, a letter dated January 5, 1982 arrived from the Canadian High Commission, Immigration Section in Nairobi giving him even better news. "We are prepared to accept your application for resettlement in Canada providing you are able to meet our medical and background check requirements." The letter told him to go see one of the approved doctors for a series of tests and medical examinations.

Ted had not been this happy and this scared at the same time in years. He was nervous that he might have picked up some disease from the poor living conditions in the refugee camp. But Ted need not have worried. He was healthy and lucky.

He went through the interview and medical process with no glitches. "I was alone, but knowing that I was going to Canada was a huge relief."

After passing his medical, Ted received another letter asking him to give the Canadian High Commission his choice of when he would like to go to Canada. He could get on a plane any time up to a year from that date, the letter told him. Ted could hardly wait. "Anytime, even tomorrow," he thought.

Ted got the required vaccinations and picked up his promissory note to book his first ride in an airplane, a flight from Nairobi to London, England. From there, he would go to Canada.

Ted finished his classes a couple of weeks later and didn't wait for the graduation. He simply left.

True to his nature, Ted shared almost everything he owned before he boarded the plane. He only had $5 U.S. in his pocket, but he really should have given all his money away.

The immigration officers had told him that if he had any money, he should not carry it with him when he left the country. Government officials were checking all non-tourists leaving Kenya in an effort to stop smuggling and make sure citizens were not taking money out of the Kenyan economy. The immigration officers had also told Ted that if something happened at the airport and he was put in prison, they could not help him.

While Ted was going through security at the airport, he was called aside and sent to a separate room. There, he was subjected to what he calls "a humiliating search." They asked him to take off his shoes and strip to his underwear.

One female and two males searched Ted but found only the $5 he had in his pants pocket. Ted quickly offered it to them. "I was worried the money would land me back in jail and I would not get to Canada. I was so afraid. This was a reminder of my traumatic past. It was another degrading experience."

The officers held him there for several terrifying minutes while his mind filled with images of horror and loss. "It was maybe five minutes, but it felt like forever."

Ted cursed himself for not listening to the immigration officials who had warned him. "I did a stupid thing. For $5, now I could lose my opportunity," he thought. "I was hating myself and blaming myself."

Finally, the woman officer said: 'Let him go. We have more people to search. It's just $5. Let him go.' It was sweet music to Ted's ears. He quickly put on his clothes and ran for the departure gate.

It was 11 o'clock at night and Ted didn't know what to think.

"When the plane was taking off, it still did not feel real. I was so happy I was leaving that troubling experience behind me and I was also wondering what was waiting for me. I felt joy, uncertainty, relief and fear. All those things were going through my mind. It was a very emotional time."

Ted was seated beside an English couple who had been on vacation in South Africa. They were kind to him and calmed him down somewhat. When the plane arrived at London's Heathrow Airport eight hours later, the couple guided Ted to the Air Canada check-in counter and bid him good luck.

It was 8 o'clock in the morning in England and the plane to Canada wouldn't leave until 5:30 in the afternoon. Ted had to make a tough decision. He only had $5 U.S. in his pocket. He was hungry but he was also anxious to feed what had grown to a two-pack-a-day smoking habit.

For a man who was used to going without food, it was an easy call to deal with his nicotine cravings before feeding his stomach, so Ted set out to find a store where he could purchase cigarettes.

He came across a woman who was handing out free cigarette samples while promoting a new brand of cigarettes. This was new territory for Ted and it took him a few minutes, with his broken English, to understand that she would give him an entire package if he tried a sample cigarette. Finally, he gratefully accepted the sample pack and walked through the giant maze that is the Heathrow Airport to find a place to buy a sandwich.

The British pound was stronger than the U.S. dollar at that time and Ted had to use almost all of his $5 to buy the cheapest sandwich he could find. He was still hungry after eating it, but had learned to survive on a small amount of food. The remaining change wouldn't even buy a drink. So Ted just sat in the departure area and read a secondhand book he picked up in Kenya to kill the time before his next flight.

At 5:30 p.m., Ted boarded an Air Canada flight from London, England to Calgary, Alberta.

All he possessed were the clothes he was wearing and a small backpack containing a couple of secondhand books, including an English dictionary and a story about South African martyr Steve Biko, one sweater, an extra shirt, one extra pair of socks, a pair of pants and one pair of underwear.

He arrived at Calgary's International Airport at 5 p.m. on Friday, March 19, 1982. He had completed the first part of his journey to his new home in Regina, Saskatchewan.

At age 27, Ted Jaleta was starting a new life.

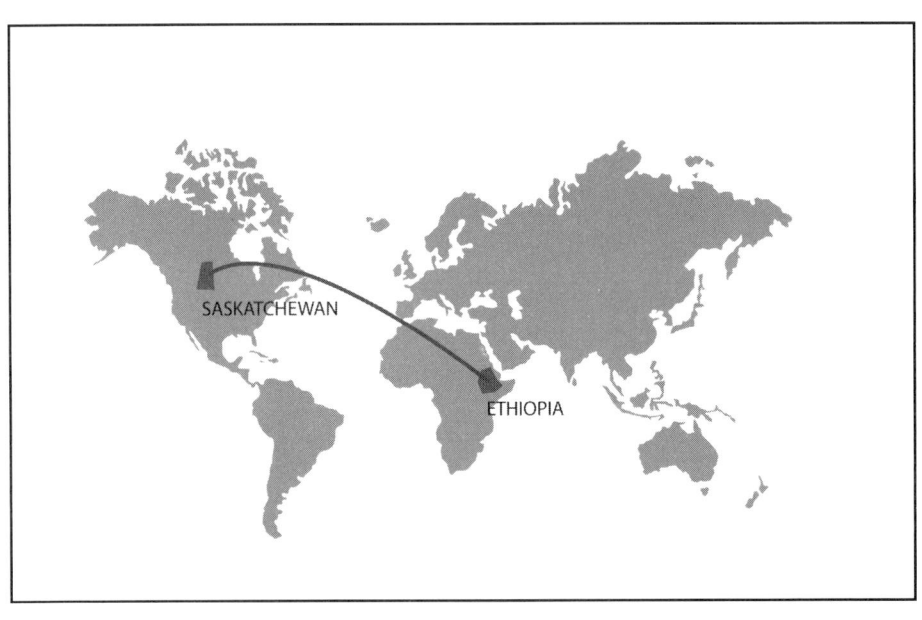

Part Two

Prologue Two

It's late spring in Saskatchewan's Qu'Appelle Valley and 50-year-old Ted Jaleta is running along the tree-lined roads that surround Echo Lake. He's competing in the Fort Qu'Appelle/Echo Lake 20-kilometre road race, enjoying the cool morning breeze.

The farmers and local residents have pulled out their lawn chairs and are sitting along the course to cheer on the runners. They all know Ted now. They know he is the best long distance runner in the province and has won this race nine times already, seven of them in a row. No one else can claim that level of success in Saskatchewan's oldest road race.

Ted thinks about how he'd like to add another win to his total today. He can almost feel the thrill of victory and the sense of accomplishment that comes with winning.

Ted thinks that his friend Christina Vuksic must be right. This race probably is what the Boston Marathon was like when it first started, with people running for fun from one spot to another among friendly faces and cheering locals.

Ted briefly wonders where Chris is in the pack behind him and then he quickly glances around to enjoy the view. This is the one of the most beautiful courses he has ever run.

Starting at the high school, runners make their way through the town of Fort Qu'Appelle and follow the road past a golf course, a provincial park and numerous cottages and homes along the lake's edge, including those on First Nations land and in a resort village. The entire course circles the lake and is lined with bushes and aspen, spruce, poplar and birch trees. Except for the lack of wildlife, the hills and water of the Qu'Appelle Valley remind him of the Ethiopian Highlands.

This race's terrain is hard for a runner, up and down hills and around twisting curves, but this road is paved – not like those of his childhood.

Ted's mind transports him back in time to the wonderful images of his youth. He can hear his sisters laughing as his younger brothers run behind him trying to catch up. The monkeys are extremely noisy today and he can see his parents visiting with neighbours while they drink their coffee.

Ted then remembers some of the positive events that have happened to him in the last 20 years. He recalls the thrill of racing against high-calibre athletes from around the world. These people started out as his heroes. Now they were his friends.

He thinks about all the people who taught him about Canada and helped him build a successful new life here. He is truly thankful, and thinking about them makes him smile.

He's had a second chance at life. A wonderful, exciting chance, and it's gone so well. In some ways, it's been even better than the awards and acknowledgements he's received for his running. These are lifelong gifts that Ted can never repay.

Then he rounds a corner on the Saskatchewan road and the sound of dozens of farmers and supporters cheering for the runners wakes him to the present, to the final leg of today's Echo Valley race.

Ted snaps back to reality and sneaks a peek behind him. No one is near.

He crosses the finish line in first place, still smiling from the memories.

This is his favourite place to run.

This is his favourite race. And he is their favourite runner.

He's a hero here. This is Canada.

And it feels great!

Chapter Seven

A New Life

Ted stepped off the plane in Calgary, Alberta, on a cool spring day, not entirely sure of what would happen next. He followed the crowd to Canada Customs and was the last person to go through security, which was, this time, not nearly as traumatic as it had been in Kenya.

Ted knew that someone from Canada's Department of Immigration should be there to meet him but, so far, no one had called his name. So he just sat down and waited. And waited.

Finally, about 30 minutes later, an immigration officer came running up to him and apologized for his tardiness. The man had actually forgotten to pick Ted up. Ted just smiled and grabbed his backpack, ready to go with the officer to do whatever was next in the plans.

They started walking outside to the car when the officer noticed that Ted was shaking and shivering. It was an unseasonably cold day in Calgary for the month of March, at about minus 7 degrees Celsius. The wind, blowing at about 30 kilometres per hour, was cooler than the more common warm-wind chinooks that regularly grace this southern Alberta city.

The temperature when Ted left Kenya was in the mid 20s. His one thin sweater wasn't nearly enough to keep his 135-lb tired, overwhelmed body warm in Canada. He wasn't cold for long, as the immigration officer loaned Ted his jacket until they got out of the wind and inside the car.

It was the first act of kindness that Ted experienced in this new country and it is one he has never forgotten. "Not many people would do that. I can recall that day clearly. I was so nervous and confused."

As they drove to an inexpensive downtown motel where Ted was to spend the night, Ted looked outside the car window in awe at the passing scenery. It was flat with a few hills and it seemed to take forever to get from the airport to the motel. The sturdy houses made of wood and brick were lined up in straight rows along paved streets here, unlike the hodge-podge of scattered houses in many areas of Addis Ababa or the makeshift shacks he left behind in Nairobi.

The immigration officer left Ted at the motel for the night with some cursory instructions along the lines of: 'When you are ready, you can order a meal and just sign for it. We'll pay for it later. In the morning, I'll come and pick you up to take you to the airport for your flight to Saskatchewan.'

Ted took a shower and then went down to the dining room to order some food. In the past 48 hours, he had only eaten the one small sandwich in London and a small meal on the plane. He was hungry, but he was also tired and confused. He became even more confused when the dining room staff told him that he couldn't order food there. He had to order from his room.

Ted didn't understand. He had been in hotels in Kenya and Ethiopia before, visiting friends who were staying there, but this was different. Very different. He couldn't figure out why they didn't want him to eat in the dining area. Were they closing for the night? Did they not want him there? What was wrong with him?

He still doesn't know why he was turned away. That night, all he knew was he was told to leave, so he did.

"I went back to my room and I was waiting for them to come to ask for my order. They didn't come, and I was embarrassed to go ask them what they meant. It was almost 10 o'clock. I was tired and confused, so I just went to bed."

In the morning, Ted woke up early. He had another shower and started looking around at his strange surroundings. He examined the telephone and was fascinated by the hotel services numbers on the phone panel. Then, he figured it out.

"That's what they meant!" So he dialed the kitchen for room service.

The person who answered the phone asked Ted what he wanted for breakfast. "The challenge was, I didn't know what kind of food they serve in Canada." The kitchen worker, who may have at one time been an immigrant to Canada himself, helpfully read the menu to Ted.

As Ted recognized words that he knew, he responded with: "Yes. That, too. That, too."

The kitchen worker paused and said: "You mean all?"

Ted answered: "Yes."

A little while later, a knock came on Ted's motel room door and in walked a room service clerk carrying the largest tray of food Ted had ever seen. It was loaded with piles of pancakes, eggs, bacon, sausages, toast and almost everything else a person could expect from a motel's breakfast menu.

Ted couldn't believe his eyes and neither could the clerk, who was quickly looking around the room for the three other people he thought must be waiting to share this platter of food.

"Both of us had a language barrier. He gave me a funny look and I was so embarrassed," recalls Ted. "I think he felt sorry for me."

After the room service clerk left the room, Ted was at a loss. "There was all this food on the platter and I didn't know what to do with it. I just had a pancake and eggs, familiar foods."

Today, when he remembers all the pancakes and other foods that had been cooked especially for him on his first full day in Canada, Ted laughs. He tells the story often to young Canadian students and immigrants to emphasize cultural differences and the abundance that is readily available in Canada yet rarely appreciated.

After Ted ate what he could stomach of his exorbitant breakfast that first morning in Calgary, he waited for his ride to the airport. Then he started doubting the conversation he had the day before with the immigration officer. Maybe he was supposed to get his own ride to the airport. Maybe the officer wasn't going to pick him up at the motel. It was all so strange and new.

The officer had forgotten about him the day before. Maybe he had forgotten again.

Ted didn't want to miss his flight, and he knew that the motel had a shuttle bus that went to the airport. So he hopped on the bus and left the motel behind. He checked in at the airport ticket counter and was lining up to board the plane when the immigration officer came running up to him, panting and sweating.

'Are you OK?' he asked Ted.

"Yes, I'm fine," came the reply. "I'm just going to board the plane." Ted then said goodbye, thanked his host and moved on to the next leg of the journey.

Ted had very little knowledge of the province that was his destination that day. "I knew they grew grain, but that's about it," he says of Saskatchewan. He would later learn that although the area around his new home, the capital city of Regina, was flat prairie surrounded by fields of wheat and other grains, the province of Saskatchewan was so much more than that.

At about half the size of Ethiopia, Saskatchewan has a varied landscape of prairie, hills, forests, lakes and rivers similar to the scenery Ted had grown up around. There are no mountains, though. Mountains in Canada are found further west in the provinces of Alberta and British Columbia. Ted would also come to appreciate that every one of the 350,000 trees[18] in Regina had been hand-planted on the grassy prairie. The trees and greenspaces, including the 930-hectare Wascana Centre[19] in the middle of the city, would make Ted's transition a tiny bit easier by reminding him of the place he was born.

* * *

When Ted arrived in Regina on that Saturday morning of March 20, 1982, he was surprised at the flatness of the landscape. Regina is only 577 metres above sea level and the only hills are small manmade mounds that are good for tobogganing fun in the wintertime. Ted couldn't believe the amount of sky he could see all around him, and he would later be surprised that Regina seems to pop up out of nowhere when driving toward it from the west.

He was met at the airport that day by Doug Sutherland, an employment counsellor at the time with Canada Employment and Immigration. Sutherland's job was to assist newly-arriving refugees in getting settled within their first year in Canada.

"He introduced himself. He called me Mr. Jaleta," recalls Ted, who was quickly impressed with this welcome to Regina. Sutherland had a $50 cheque for Ted and took him straight to a bank to cash it. Ted was then asked to sign some papers and was relieved when Sutherland drove him to a local motel to get some rest. He told Ted he'd be back to pick him up on Monday morning to fill out more forms and get him further established.

It was the weekend and Ted didn't know anyone. He was tired and unsure of his surroundings and uncomfortable. He didn't eat at all that day and went straight to bed. He slept the rest of Saturday and woke up Sunday morning around 9:30.

The weather in Regina on that March morning was "kind of nice," remembers Ted, who decided to get some fresh air and check out his surroundings from the balcony of his second-floor motel room. Unfortunately, the motel room's door automatically locked from the outside when it was closed, and Ted was left standing outside in what very quickly turned from 'nice' to 'freezing' weather for a transplanted African who was not wearing a jacket.

He stood there for at least half an hour until a cleaning lady came by and asked him if he was OK. She unlocked Ted's door and showed him what had happened, giving him detailed instructions to make sure he didn't get locked outside again.

Once Ted had warmed up in his motel room, he decided to face the challenge of ordering food in Canada. There was a restaurant attached to the motel, so he went there to eat.

He was nervous, especially after his incident in the Calgary motel, so he ordered the only foods he recognized on the menu as a possible main course meal: "Chicken and rice." It was 10:30 in the morning. The waitress hesitated and then agreed to place the order for him. Ted ate his food and when it came time to pay for his meal, he was again clueless.

"I had no idea of the amount I owed. I went and held out my hands and showed her all the money I had. 'Oh,' she said. 'No, this is the amount.' And she took the right amount from me."

Ted was scared to go back to the restaurant again that day, so he went to bed that night without any supper. "I only ate once on Sunday. I didn't have the energy to put myself through such a challenging experience again."

On Monday morning, he gathered up his courage and walked in to the restaurant for breakfast. The same waitress who had helped him before was working that shift, which made him a little more comfortable in these new surroundings.

She asked him if he knew much about Regina and visited with him as she had likely done with other newcomers to Canada. When he tried to order chicken and rice again, she gently explained that: 'In Canada, it's too early in the day to eat that. I'll order you a good breakfast.'

"Her name was Rita, I remember. She helped me learn what a normal breakfast was in Canada. She said: 'Today's breakfast is on me. You don't have to pay.' That's one of the first positive experiences I had in Regina."

Later that morning, Doug Sutherland arrived to take Ted to complete the paperwork and go to the Regina Open Door Society, the agency responsible for finding apartments and essential living items for new immigrants.

Ted went with Open Door Society staff to the Army and Navy department store and purchased essentials such as cutlery, dishes, pots and bedding. Ted also bought his first winter coat there, which came in handy later that year when he first experienced snow.

He had seen pictures of snow before he came to Canada while watching 'Western' television, but he really had no idea what it was like. "It doesn't snow in Ethiopia. There is some snow on the tops of some of the tallest mountains, but there is no word for snow in our language. I used to see those Western movies and I was so fascinated by that white stuff. We have some rivers in my region with white sand on the banks of the rivers. I thought this snow was even more beautiful than that."

Ted's first real-life experience with snow wasn't quite as picture perfect as he had seen on the television, though.

"I didn't know it was so cold," he laughs.

* * *

About a week after arriving in Saskatchewan, the Regina Open Door Society found Ted a simple suite in a house on Victoria Avenue, just west of the city's downtown. "When Ted came, the vacancy rate was half of one per cent. Some of the accommodations we had weren't prime," recalls Sutherland.

The room was on the second floor of a house that had tenants above and below him. He had a small twin-size bed, a small refrigerator and an ugly brown couch with burn marks on it. There was no television and no telephone. Just the essentials.

There was no running water in Ted's room. He had to wash his dishes in a washroom down the hall that he shared with the upstairs tenants. "At the time, I thought it was normal," he says of these arrangements. A suite to himself was considerably better than what he had in the last two places he had lived.

The only highlight of his room was the window facing out on to Victoria Avenue, which runs east to west through the city's downtown. This section of Victoria Avenue is one of the more memorable pieces of road for newcomers to Regina. The branches of large American elm trees drape over the street here to meet in the middle of the boulevard, creating a majestic canopy.

The only wildlife Ted would see for the next few years in his new city were the occasional wild rabbit or squirrel running across the grass, or a muskrat swimming in Wascana Creek, which trickles in and away from Wascana Lake at the city's core. Occasionally, a moose or deer might mistakenly wander into town to be chased down and safely transported outside the city limits again but, mostly, Ted had to get used to the noises of his human neighbours replacing the constant bantering of the monkeys and other animals he had encountered in Africa.

There were a few drug users who lived upstairs from Ted. They mistakenly assumed that all black people used drugs. When they asked Ted if he had any drugs for them, they were surprised when he told them: 'No, I don't do drugs.' His neighbours weren't the only ones to make that assumption in the early 1980s.

"A few times, I was stopped on the street as well. Sometimes I was even asked if I wanted to make extra money by selling drugs."

Ted, of course, turned down those offers. He found it disturbing to be bothered in this way but tried not to let it irritate him too much. He decided this was to be his new home and he would do his best to adapt. He knew that poor choices could ruin his chances in Canada. He also knew that getting involved in drugs was a bad choice and he would not allow himself to be led astray down that path.

Doug Sutherland says there were many challenges facing newcomers in those days. Many immigrants were stereotyped and others tried to take advantage of them because of their lack of confidence in their new surroundings. Sutherland's advice to his immigrant clients then was always: "Walk away. Chances are, wherever you go, someone will taunt you. There will be lots of challenges," he warned.

"When I remember Ted in those days, he was always positive, optimistic," says Sutherland. "He was anxious to make a good start, to make some friends. When he came to Regina, he was a wide-eyed new resident of Canada with lots of optimism. And he was a little shy."

Part of Ted's shyness was because of the unfamiliar environment. Part of it came from still being in survival mode, traumatized by his past and uncertain about his future.

"I was not sure if other people would accept me. I was not quite out of day-to-day survival mentality. I had survival skills but I didn't have anyone to rely on. Here, I felt like an orphan. I just had to be tough and accept the reality."

"Ted stood out as one of those most likely to succeed," says Sutherland of the many immigrants he assisted in those years. "He had a great deal of optimism. He wasn't carrying a lot of baggage. When he arrived, he made a conscious decision this is what he wanted to do. And always, he had a smile. Many immigrants came with very heavy hurts, having left many family members behind. Some came with the family members left on the beaches of Vietnam, floating face down. It was not a good time," Sutherland says of those years.

* * *

Shortly after arriving in Regina, Ted had to attend 'Welcome to Canada' classes through the Regina Open Door Society. There, he listened to speakers from several different community groups, including the local government and Regina Police Service. It was an enlightening but also troubling experience for him.

"When I saw law enforcement figures, I was not seeing the Canadian police officers in my mind. I was seeing the police who brutalized us and forced us to give them bribes."

Ted still has difficulty today at times automatically accepting that men and women who wear police or security uniforms are there to protect the public. When police cars pull up behind him, he has difficulty keeping his heart from racing. "It takes me back in my mind to the torment of the authorities in Africa. Subconsciously, my mind goes there."

Ted has worked hard to overcome that distrust of authority. Some of his best friends today are Canadian police officers. He has participated in several police-sponsored running events and has even helped Royal Canadian Mounted Police recruits with a running clinic.

Another one of the speakers at Ted's 'Welcome to Canada' classes in 1982 was an employee from Revenue Canada who talked about how adults in Canada must fill out income tax forms each year. This was a foreign concept to Ted. "What is income tax?" he wondered. "Any taxes due in Ethiopia are paid through payroll deduction. That's all. My first income tax filing in Canada took me about two days to do," Ted recalls with a laugh.

* * *

Every country is only as welcoming or as kind as its worst resident, and Canada is no exception. While Canada Employment and Immigration staff could help Ted write a resume and offer him ideas on where to find a job in his field of graphic arts, they couldn't step in to make sure that he would always be treated fairly or compassionately in this new environment.

Shortly after arriving in Regina, Ted saw a graphic arts job advertised in the newspaper. He went by the office to drop off his resume and was asked to start work the following Monday.

There were about 10 people in the print shop. Ted did camera work, hot metal plates and paste-ups. "One of the challenges at the time was not my ability to perform my work. I worked very hard, sometimes too hard to please them. It was the interaction in social gatherings that gave me the most difficulty," he says.

Ted could not relate to this strange new Canadian culture in a way that made him fit in quickly. His co-workers talked about playing football and asked him to join them for a fun game on the weekend. 'Football' is 'soccer' everywhere except in North America, so Ted showed up carrying a soccer ball. "They laughed at me. They made me feel so small. Maybe they didn't mean to," adds the ever-forgiving Ted.

Despite his discomfort, Ted tried to participate in the game he didn't understand. The other players had grown up with stereotypes of African Americans being great football stars. They incorrectly thought that Ted was one of those. "They assumed I could catch the ball because I am black," chuckles Ted. "I could run, but I couldn't catch."

Ted also had trouble fitting in on Monday mornings. When his co-workers shared stories about what they had done on the weekends, he had nothing to contribute to the conversation. His social life was quite limited compared to theirs.

He was busy concentrating on adjusting, keeping himself employed and paying his bills so he could stay in this new country. He had an interest-free loan of about $800 that he had to pay back to the Canadian government for his airfare to come to Canada. Keeping a job was imperative.

It was more difficult than he imagined.

"I started at that print shop in May but at the end of that month, I was called in to the office by one of the owners. I was fired."

'You appear troubled emotionally and you need to deal with it,' the boss told him. Ted grabbed his jacket and left.

One of the other workers in the print shop was a woman who had come to Canada from Eastern Europe. She had befriended Ted and she caught up with him outside the building. 'Now that you have left, I have to tell you something,' she said. 'They think you have some kind of psychological problem.'

It was a painful message for Ted to hear and one he didn't understand. He was confused and worried about his future, and started to doubt himself. Maybe he was incapable of doing his job. Maybe he couldn't function in Canada.

He went to visit a fellow refugee to talk about what happened. It was a temporary comfort that was enough to help him move on. Although that first job ended in an emotionally-devastating experience, Ted was determined to succeed in Canada. "I went through a lot of bumpy roads to immerse into Canadian society," he recalls. "It was quite painful the first couple of years."

Instead of waiting for another job to come to him, Ted looked for work on his own. He went to the local Temporary Manpower office and took any job he could get, even if only for a few hours at a time. He cleaned up house construction worksites and loaded chickens on a truck at a poultry farm near the city's outskirts. Anything to earn some money.

Ted didn't consider applying for social assistance, the provincial subsidy given to low-income unemployed or unemployable individuals. He didn't even know where the Social Services office was, and says it did not even cross his mind then. He wanted to make it in Canada on his own.

A couple of weeks later, Ted walked by a photo lab and saw a sign looking for someone to process film during the night shift. He was willing to take any job, and this one was within walking distance of his apartment and better-paying than the first job.

"It was mostly a positive experience. I received a paycheque and I didn't have to depend on others for support. But the social challenges were still there."

Ted was still feeling very alone.

A few months after arriving in Regina, he got sick with a bad flu and went to a medical centre to get antibiotics. Ted had an allergic reaction to the medication, but he didn't know that at the time. He had a terrible case of diarrhea and his stomach was bleeding. He phoned a taxi to take him to the hospital but was so weak from dehydration that he could barely walk to the cab. The taxi driver asked him if he was on drugs or drunk.

At the hospital emergency unit, the staff asked Ted for his next of kin. He answered truthfully: "I have none. I am new to this country and I have no one."

He recalls seeing sadness on the nurse's face. "I had no knowledge of what to do or who to call."

The emergency room staff kept him in the hospital overnight for observation. They treated him with intravenous fluids to re-hydrate his body, took him off the offending antibiotics and gave him instructions on how to get over his illness.

"At the time, I could only rely on myself. I didn't have any choice until I met some other immigrants and we learned to look after each other."

Through the Open Door Society, Ted met several people who had just arrived from Africa and elsewhere. "A few came from Ethiopia. Some were also from Eastern European countries. One thing we had in common was loneliness."

The group found they needed each other's support even more when, a few months later, an immigrant who had come to Regina from Somalia was killed in a bizarre attack one evening after he went to a bar with some unsavoury characters. They all went to his funeral and decided they would not go alone to unfamiliar places. "We had to learn to be careful."

Unfortunately for Ted, one of the most dangerous places he had to go was the place where he worked.

Ted didn't talk much in those early days, especially about his past. He was still deeply troubled by it and thought that no one would believe him or other refugees who came from a similar background.

"It sounds like fiction," he says of his story. "I did not think anyone would care to listen to me. When sharing my deepest feelings of my past, I expect someone to listen."

Ted couldn't bear to take the chance that others would not believe him or, even worse, would ridicule him for the pain he continued to experience. So he mostly kept his stories to himself, doing his job at work and ignoring the jeers of fellow workers and other people who were unkind to him.

A low point in Ted's new life in Canada came when he was working at the photo lab. He had gone into the large walk-in cooler to do inventory on some supplies when a co-worker slammed the large steel door shut, trapping Ted inside with no method of escape for several frightening minutes.

"It was dark. I couldn't see, but I could feel my eyelashes were covered in frost. I thought I was going to die. It was a terrifying experience," he says, still shuddering at the thought.

Ted pounded again and again on the steel door but no one opened it. There was no window, so he couldn't see out and the persons on the other side couldn't see how he was faring inside the cooler. Finally, Leigh Burton, a co-worker, came along and asked the men standing at the cooler door what they were doing. Once they told him, Burton reprimanded them for their stupid trick and made them release Ted from his freezing prison.

The memories of that incident trigger a pain-filled sob from Ted.

"Upsetting. Embarrassing. Humiliating. Painful," he says of the cooler incident.

Ted didn't get angry with the men that day. "I wish I knew what was going on in their minds. I was glad Leigh was there to free me. There was no apology from them. They continued to taunt me and make fun of me."

Ted has come up with some reasons why the men may have behaved in that way.

"Maybe they were inexperienced with different cultures and intolerant of others who were not like them. The way we treat people reflects the way we feel about ourselves. If our self-esteem is low, we might try to bring others down to compensate for our lack of self-confidence."

In any case, Ted is still not interested in blaming those men or the owner of the now-closed lab. It happened and it is over. The sad part for him is that it can happen anywhere.

"Every country has individuals and groups within it that give the country a bad name. Every country has a weakness and a dark part in its history. I was new. I didn't know normal behaviour in this country. I was probably not acting or behaving the way they expected and I was quiet and reserved. I was just doing what I was told."

On another occasion, a different co-worker overheard Ted's supervisor making a bet with others that the supervisor could get Ted to go downstairs and clean the sewage that had backed up in the basement. Ted was just 'a slave' who could be ordered around, the man bragged to his friends. The co-worker went up to Ted and told him what he overheard. Ted followed his advice and rejected the supervisor's order as not being in his job description.

The supervisor was reprimanded the next day for his inappropriate remarks and racist slurs, but the complaint that got the man in trouble had come from someone other than Ted.

Ted would rather take the abuse than complain. He was scared of losing his job and made every effort to please his bosses. "I had already lost one job. I had to be quiet and believe that it would get better," he says.

"When we come to this country as newcomers, we come with a great hope. We faced so much adversity before we came here. Before I arrived, I realized that things would not be handed to me on a silver platter and that I would have to work hard. I did not expect that some people would treat me so badly, however. When you face individuals and groups that do these negative things towards you, it's a setback. You wonder if you are in the right place. If you are not strong, you cannot survive."

He has sadly watched other newcomers to Canada give up the fight to fit in. "Such a negative experience could trigger segregation. That's why some of the immigrants tend to stick together when they feel rejected. Segregation may restrict their opportunities."

Ted tried to focus instead on spending time with co-workers like Leigh Burton and a woman named Trudy who had come from Germany. Trudy's ethnic group also faced racism when she first arrived in Canada. She was called derogatory terms such as 'DP,' which stands for 'displaced person.'

Trudy told Ted about some of the negative experiences she had when she first came. She was also a good cook and invited him to her family's home for a wonderful homemade meal. "Those kinds of good people and their actions gave me hope."

As a child in Africa and an adult in Canada, Ted has faced these challenges and is certain there will be more in his future as well. But he tries not to let it bother him.

"I don't see myself as a coloured person or different than anyone else. I've never felt black or different in my life. I'm not denying that I am black. I don't see it as a problem. I see myself as a whole person. Everybody has weaknesses and strengths. If somebody sees me differently, that's not a problem with me. That's their problem."

Ted says he was raised not to be deterred by whatever challenges he faces. "Don't be diminished by them. When I am treated badly by people, I like to show them I am not the person they think."

Ted could handle abusive comments thrown at him from total strangers on the street, but being abused in the workplace is in a different category. Some of his most painful memories of his first years in Canada revolve around when his supervisor and co-workers were harassing him.

"I used to worry each morning about what I would face that day. I tried to hide it but it was one of the most distressing times of my life. It was more emotionally devastating than when I got tortured, because it was so demeaning to my soul. In the prison, I knew what I had done to cause that abuse. Here, I do not know to this day."

For Ted, emotional scars are worse than physical pain. He has a clear message for individuals who are in a position of authority: "You have absolute power to affect your neighbours, friends and community. You can cripple and demoralize others or you can use your power in a positive manner. You have a great opportunity to do the right thing."

* * *

In December 1982, Ted was about to celebrate his first Christmas in Canada. Alone. Fortunately, Leigh Burton invited him to go to Saskatoon, about two hours north of Regina, to spend Christmas with Leigh and his parents and siblings. Ted gratefully accepted the offer.

The home of Carl and Fay Burton had always had an open-door policy, welcoming all visitors and friends invited in by their four sons. They often invited university students to spend the holidays with them and Fay relished the role of feeding and entertaining a large crowd, because of her upbringing in a large farm family.

"People came and went without invitation," explains Fay. But Ted was different. He made a lasting impression, especially on her.

"He never gave up. He was always striving ahead, for that ultimate goal, in spite of all the duress and discrimination. And principles! He's a remarkable young man."

Ted and Fay developed a bond that would last the rest of their lives.

"I was the one that kept the connection with Ted. I guess he saw me as a mother figure," says Fay. "He could talk to me. I was interested in how he got out of Ethiopia. I was interested in the language, his life, trying to fathom what he went through and how they lived. It was as much a culture shock for me to look in on an Ethiopian situation as it was for Ted to spend Christmas with us."

The Burtons exchanged gifts that Christmas morning in 1982 and Ted was included in that tradition. It was strange compared to the Christmas rituals he had experienced in Ethiopia. "On Christmas Eve at home, we would go to church for midnight mass and then everybody would get together for a big feast. There's no gift exchange."

He recalls the "warm, nice family" he saw in the Burton home and how it touched him emotionally that first Christmas. "I had not had that kind of warm family gathering since I left my home country. I barely managed to control my emotions."

But Ted did feel slightly uncomfortable when the family started calling out names for the gift opening. He had forgotten to ask about Christmas traditions in Canada and felt bad that he had not brought anything with him from Regina. All of a sudden, one of the family members handed Ted a gift and said: 'Here's yours.' Ted couldn't believe it.

"They knew I played soccer and they gave me a soccer ball," Ted grins. "I still have that soccer ball."

One of the funnier moments of that first Canadian Christmas for Ted came during the special Christmas meal. The dining area was packed with a lot of action as the bowls of food were passed back and forth between herself and Carl, their four boys and Ted. "You know how you talk louder and louder to somebody who doesn't speak the language well?" asks Fay. "Well, I had Ted on my right side and so the conversation with Ted got louder and louder because he didn't know what turnip was and that kind of thing, so we had to explain these foods. As I got louder, Leigh tapped me on the shoulder and said: 'Mom, Ted doesn't have a hearing problem. He has a language problem.' " Fay still laughs about her way of over-compensating that day to help this newcomer fit in.

After that first visit, Ted was like another member of the Burton family. "I called them mom and dad," he says of Fay and Carl. Ted travelled to their home in Saskatoon on weekends or summer breaks for the next several years and was welcome there whether they were home or not. About the only time he wasn't comfortable in the Burton home was at Christmas.

"It was different for Ted," explains Fay. "That's why after two or three Christmases, Ted decided he wouldn't be with us. He was given gifts and he wasn't used to gift exchanges. We were extravagant at

Christmas with the guys and they were with us. It was too commercialized for Ted. It was just a different society, different customs."

Ted did enjoy his new relationship with the Burtons and he says they taught him a lot about Canadian culture. "They were patient with me. Fay is wonderful. When I need to talk with someone I can trust, to truly express my feelings, I pick up the phone and call her."

It is one of the few long-lasting, completely-trusting relationships Ted has been able to build in all his time in Canada.

Chapter Eight

Second Chance

On Sunday mornings for most of his first year in Regina, Ted went to a local restaurant with some immigrant friends to have "breakfast and a smoke." They lamented about their past and didn't hold out much hope for their future.

By mid-1983, Ted became tired of this routine. He decided he was done rehashing the events of Ethiopia and that he needed to make radical changes to create a more positive life for himself.

"When immigrants come to this country, it's a tough and often painful transition. To move forward, they should try to cut themselves off from the negative parts of their past and look to the future," he believes.

He went for long walks in nearby Wascana Centre and started re-examining what might make him feel better about himself. He decided that he needed to quit smoking and start running again.

Ted had seen people running in the park and found that he was quickly welcomed into the group when he took up the sport again. Some of the runners were interested in where he was from and invited him to join them on a regular basis. "I started running with them every Sunday morning instead of going to the restaurant with my immigrant friends."

Getting back into running was much easier for Ted than it was to stop smoking. He tried to quit on his own, without success, and then went to a doctor to get a prescription for nicotine gum. He hated the taste of the gum and chewed it for only a few weeks, deciding it cost too much and he was only using it as an excuse. He needed a good reason to stop.

Ted wrote a letter to a friend in the United States and asked him why he thought Ted was having trouble kicking the nicotine habit. The friend reminded Ted about all the adversity he had already come through and encouraged him to keep trying. 'After all that, are you saying you can't overcome this urge?' the friend questioned.

Ted took specific measures to help him stop smoking. For a year, he stopped drinking coffee, wine and the occasional beer. He found that alcohol and caffeine gave him more desire to smoke. "Especially caffeine. A cigarette goes very well with that. The struggle for me was after meals when I missed cigarettes the most."

He even avoided places where he knew others would be smoking. "One of the keys to success in quitting smoking is to not compromise your health by being with people who don't care for their own health."

Ted had cigarette cravings for almost a year. It was quite a struggle, but he is glad he won that battle. In the process, he became a smoker's worst nightmare.

"After a year, I became a very radical advocate against smoking. Now I hate smoking. It just drives me crazy. It smells awful."

He recalls an incident after one Sunday morning run when he and some friends went to a restaurant for breakfast. They were annoyed to find a female customer beside them, puffing on a cigarette in the non-smoking section. Ted tried to express his displeasure with his body language but nothing happened. Finally, he complained to the manager, who asked the woman to stop or move to the smoking section, which she did.

Years later, Ted met that woman again, when she hired him for a job. She recognized him from that day in the restaurant and still teases him that he is lucky she even hired him. She and Ted are now good friends. Better yet, the woman has since stopped smoking as well.

* * *

During his first few years in Canada, Ted also tried to improve himself to fit in better with Canadian society. An example of his determination could be seen in his daily reading of the dictionary.

That's right. The dictionary.

He took a copy of this unusual reading choice to work each day and memorized entries during coffee and lunch breaks. At night, he kept it on his bedside table so he could read from it each evening before going to sleep.

He did this every day. For a year.

He wanted to improve his English skills and he set a goal of memorizing 20 to 30 words every day. "Not all of them sank in," says Ted, almost apologetically. "I was able to learn five or 10 a day."

During one lunch break, a co-worker at the photo lab asked Ted what he was reading, wondering if it was the Bible. Ted was embarrassed to show him the book, thinking at the time, and probably rightfully so, that any admission of his inadequacies might diminish his credibility in the workplace. When he told the co-worker that it was a dictionary, he then had to answer the next question: 'Why?'

"I had a desire to learn the language," says Ted about those days. "Each night I read some words, wrote down the meanings, memorized them and then went back to the book. I learned the origins of the language and how those words were formed."

Ted's efforts to learn English have helped him considerably in Canada but he is easily frustrated that he still has some difficulty with spoken English. It is a terrible burden for a perfectionist. He is eloquent in four Ethiopian languages and knows some Arabic and Swahili from when he was in Sudan and Kenya.

Ted is an eager listener who learns from each conversation and experience, and speaks carefully with considerable thought and emotion behind each sentence. He also has an exceptional knowledge of world politics, history and events. Ted watches the news on television while he drinks his morning coffee and visits the library daily to read newspapers from around the world.

John Bolstad, a runner who works as a draftsman, met Ted in 1983 when he began running at the Douglas Park outdoor track in east Regina. The two men began training together a couple times a week. "I've never known such a guy, very committed in his beliefs and values," says Bolstad. "He appreciates life here in Regina. He doesn't always think the grass is greener on the other side of the street."

Bolstad credits Ted, who is 10 years his senior, for helping him to see possibilities and struggles from a larger-world view. Bolstad's wife is originally from the Philippines, and Ted always knows something about whatever world situation is being discussed, says Bolstad, whose parents and siblings also began to call Ted their friend shortly after meeting him. "It's always interesting to talk to him. Now, he has caught up and surpassed our knowledge of world affairs. He was always a good listener. He learns from other people, whether they make good or bad decisions."

While trying to adapt to Canada, Ted was careful to avoid anything that might endanger his refugee status. Fay Burton recalls sitting in their Saskatoon backyard one night in 1984 with Ted and other family members after an evening meal. They saw a young man in the alley try to break in to a neighbour's house by throwing a rock at the patio door.

"Our son took off after him on the bicycle and Ted went out to be with our son. Then all of a sudden, Ted came back. He said to me: 'I could have outrun him and caught him but I have to be very careful. I'm new here,'" recalls Fay.

Ted was extremely thankful he was even alive to this point. The chances for survival were so slim. He wanted to keep moving forward in this new country.

Ted isn't sure if there were angels or some spiritual power or divine intervention involved in saving his life. "Maybe somebody is protecting me. Maybe there's a supernatural force. I don't know. I believe in miracles, but you have to be able to help make those happen. My chance to die was greater than to survive. In a war, some die and some live."

Ted considers himself lucky to have been shot only in the leg, and he knows his own actions determined his survival as well.

"One of my strengths is that I am always decisive. When you are decisive, your chances of winning or surviving are greater. When I make a decision, even if it means following a difficult path, I stick with it."

Ted believes there are no shortcuts in life. You have to work hard, and you have to be patient and watch that work pay off.

* * *

From the moment he received his acceptance letter to immigrate to Canada, Ted had been looking forward to the day he could become a Canadian citizen. He wanted a place he could really call home, and he had no desire to leave the small city of Regina to find it.

Ted liked the fact that Regina had only about 163,000 residents at that time. He could get around without a car and felt he could adjust more quickly to a new culture if he was in a smaller centre like Regina. Some of his acquaintances went to Toronto or Vancouver to see more people of the same ethnic background, but Ted wasn't concerned about that. He knew he could blend in anywhere.

Ted carefully calculated the days that were left before he could meet the citizenship requirement of being in Canada for three years. He could hardly wait to step before a citizenship officer and be sworn in as a new Canadian. "I did not have a country I could call my own. Having citizenship reassured me of where I belonged."

A few months before his eligible date, he filled out an application form and studied the information provided about Canadian history and geography. He knew that Canada was created in 1867, Canada Day is celebrated on July 1, and that Queen Elizabeth II is Canada's Head of State, among other details tested on the multiple-choice citizenship exam. He read over the Oath of Citizenship and memorized the Canadian national anthem.

On March 26, 1985, exactly three years and eight days after arriving in Canada, Ted put on his best dress clothes and made his way to the downtown Canadian Citizenship office for the big event. As he sat listening to the citizenship officer speak about the freedoms and rights that come with living in a democratic nation, Ted looked around him at the dozen or so other immigrants from Poland, China and Vietnam. He didn't know anyone else in the room except for one Ethiopian immigrant who came that day to take a picture of Ted, as a new Canadian standing beside an RCMP officer dressed in the well-known red serge uniform.

When Ted received his citizenship papers and commemorative pin, it was an exciting and somewhat melancholy moment.

"I was very happy. This is a country I chose in my heart. I strongly believe I made the right decision to come here. It was a priceless gift to become a Canadian citizen. Canada gave me a second chance."

On the other hand, he missed his family and wondered if he would ever see them again. His new citizenship papers gave him a glimpse of hope that it still might be possible, some day. He had to be strong.

The war in Ethiopia had taken away almost 10 years of Ted's life. It had eliminated most of the carefree moments he could have had as a teenager as well as his opportunities for a post-secondary education and a successful athletic career. Canadian citizenship gave Ted an opportunity to regroup, to establish a so-called 'normal' life, to have a job and perhaps even a family of his own. "I now have a place I can call my country and home. I have a Canadian passport. I can now go anywhere I want," he recalls thinking that day.

Those who are born in Canada seldom consider this last benefit, but to a refugee, it is crucial. "People take that freedom for granted. If you lose your citizenship, you are losing your whole being."

A few months later, Ted's optimism for reconnecting with his family was revived. He had not been in contact with his parents or siblings since he left Ethiopia in 1978. He sent them a letter in 1984 telling them that he had survived his exile and was alive and living in Canada. They did not believe it was true. They thought he was dead.

Ted's family knew he and the other men had escaped to Sudan but they didn't know anything that happened after that. "That was very tough for me to think I may have lost them forever. I missed them so much."

Ethiopia was still in turmoil politically in 1984 and Ted's family was worried the letter they had received was a political ploy that might eventually lead them to harm. A friend of Ted's convinced him to try again to contact his family in 1985, this time with a tape-recorded message.

A Canadian nurse who was passing through Regina would be visiting Ethiopia in the next few weeks, the friend told him, and she would take a taped message from Ted to his family. Ted was excited about the possibility. On the tape, Ted spoke about the area where he grew up and the games they played as children. He named all his siblings and talked about events and details that only his family would know.

Only upon receipt of this tape did Ted's family celebrate the good news. "It brought peace to my family when they found out I was alive. I was so happy to hear from them after that."

Ted started corresponding with his family, usually with only simple messages of greetings and gladness because mail was still being intercepted. The messages usually went to Ted's youngest brother, who was attending college in a different province and could pass the messages on to Ted's parents without fear of government interference.

* * *

By running regularly with the runners he met in the park in his first few years in Regina, Ted accomplished his goals of making new friends and improving his own health. He didn't even mind when some of the people he used to hang out with teased him about his new pastime. "Some of my friends asked: 'Are you trying to be some kind of a track star? You are too old.'"

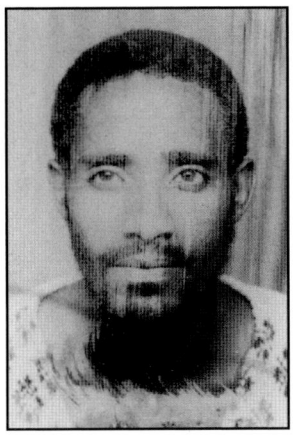

Left: A few weeks after arriving in Sudan as a refugee. 1978.

Below: Ted's first Christmas in Canada, with the Burton family. Saskatoon, Saskatchewan, 1982.

Above: Ted's brother-in-law in his police uniform with Ted. Ethiopia, 1973.

Above: Ted with his work supervisor during his internship at the Weekly Review. Nairobi, Kenya, 1981.

Above right: Chatting on the phone with friends from his second apartment in Regina. 1982.

Right: Standing in a park near downtown Regina. 1983.

Left: Ted's mother (second from right in back row) with some of Ted's siblings and nephews and nieces (front). Ethiopia, 1984.

Below: Ted proudly becomes a Canadian citizen. Regina, March 1985.

Above: Ted's sister Sadate with her husband and daughter. Ethiopia, 1986.

Above right: Competing in a 3000M indoor race. Saskatoon, 1986.

Below: Enjoying baby Adam. March 1987.

Below right: Crossing the finish line first in the CIBC Half Marathon. Winnipeg, 1988.

Above: Running through Wascana Centre park. Regina, late 1980s.

Above left: Dressed to run in Regina winters. 1988.

Right: Being interviewed by the radio station after his win in the C Fox Trot 8K race. Vancouver, British Columbia. July 1989.

Left: Staying with the front runners in the Banff Citizen 10K race. Banff, Alberta, 1990.

Below left: Accepting his award for winning the Nipawin Northern Pine 10K race. Nipawin, Saskatchewan, July 1990.

Below: The first leg of the Jasper-Banff relay. July, 1991.

Left: Winning the Downtown Dash. Regina, August 1991.
(Photo: Roy Antal, Regina Leader-Post)

Right: Father and son. 1992.

Below: Fishing in the North Saskatchewan River. Nipawin, Saskatchewan, 1992.

Above: Adam couldn't believe it when his dad came in second. Fieldhouse, Regina, 1992.

Above: Ted has won the Fort Qu'Appelle/Echo Lake road race a record 11 times. Seen here on the course in 1993, running toward his sixth of seven consecutive wins.

Left: After the Echo Lake road race with (left to right) Darren Burrows, Jason Warick, Eric Thauberger and son Adam, holding his dad's trophy. 1992.

Above left: The mountains and hills of Banff, Alberta, remind Ted of Ethiopia. 1992.

Above: Adam and Ted playing a game of Mastermind. December 1993.

Left: After the Wascana relay. Regina, 1996.

Below: Setting the Canadian Half-Marathon Masters record. Las Vegas, Nevada. February 1997.

Above left: U.S. Olympian Frank Shorter and Ted, International Masters runners. Boulder, Colorado, 1996.

Left: Ted with Keith Klockow of Regina and British Olympian Steve Jones (far right). Tampa, Florida, 1997.

Right: Ted on a running trail/road in the hills near Addis Ababa, Ethiopia. 1999.

Above: Ted with two of his brothers. Ethiopia, 1999.

Left (top to bottom) A forest near Addis Ababa, where Ethiopian national team athletes run. 1999.

Ted and his father surrounded by members of their family. 1999.

Ted on a hill overlooking Addis Ababa. 1999.

A modern-day school in a setting similar in landscape to where Ted lived in his early years. 1999.

Below: Ted retires from competitive running. September 2000. (Photo: Bryan Schlosser, Regina Leader-Post)

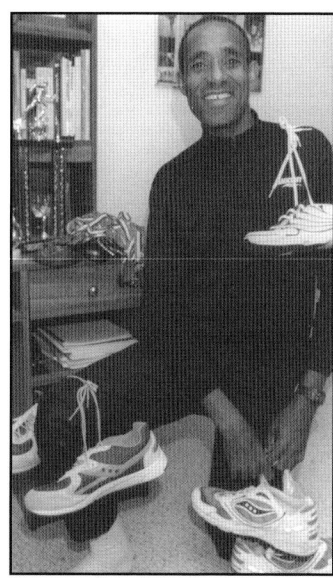

Left: Ted's last appearance in an international race, where he bid farewell to running friends and race organizers. Bloomsday 12K Run. Spokane, Washington, 2001.

Below: Ted accepts the Queen's Golden Jubilee Medal for significant contributions to Canadian society through his work. 2002.

Above: Adam at the Saskatchewan Legislature grounds. Regina, 2002.

Left: Adam on his way to earning more points toward his high school's provincial basketball championship win. Regina, 2004.

Right: Adam graduates from Grade 12. Regina, 2004.

Left: Ted is inducted into the Saskatchewan Sports Hall of Fame. Regina, June 2005.

Below left: Jill Rodgers, Ted, Chris Vuksic and Marion Craig at the Hall of Fame induction. Regina, 2005.

Below: Ted with some of his athletes (Centre: Marion Craig and Jill Rodgers standing and Chris Vuksic in front). (Photo: Roy Antal, Regina Leader-Post. June 2005.)

Far left: Sandy Bain, Curtis Koskie, Alicia Roske and Ted at the University of Regina indoor track. 2006.

Left: Ted and Regina Symphony Orchestra conductor Victor Sawa at the Beat Beethoven Run. 2006

Left: Signing autographs after addressing a school assembly. Regina, 2006.

Right: Receiving the torch from a Marion McVeety School student for the Regina leg of the World Harmony Run. Regina, 2006.

At 29 years of age, Ted was indeed past his prime for being a medallist, or so most people thought, including Ted. He simply wanted to learn about Canadian society and make connections for more job opportunities. It never crossed his mind that he might compete and win races.

Several months after he started running in the park, some of the others convinced him to join them in the upcoming charitable 10K Terry Fox Run in Regina. It was less than a shining moment in Ted's running career.

The run was two times around Wascana Centre and Ted barely made it through the first lap. He started walking the second lap and finally cut that lap in half, taking a shortcut across the grass to sit down. He had not run for almost 12 years and was also out of breath from the effects of smoking.

In May 1985, Ted ran his first official race in Canada. It was the Mini-Marathon in Moose Jaw, a city about 70 kilometres west of Regina. He finished poorly there as well.

It was a 10-kilometre race at the Canadian Air Force base south of the city. Ted started strong and sprinted with the front runners for about 100 metres. Then he slowed down considerably. He had used everything he had and his lungs were burning. The majority of the runners then passed him and by the time he reached the halfway mark, the front runners were approaching the finish line. When Ted crossed the finish line, the winner of the race had cooled down and was already dressed.

Ted had not run an entire race in more than a decade and he was not the Ted Jaleta of old who could beat everyone around him. "I still thought I could run fast, but my body was telling me I was out of shape. I needed to condition myself. The third-place female caught me with about 100 metres to go. She just smoked me."

He had never been beaten by that many people, including that many women, who are usually physically slower than men. So he joined the YMCA and decided to take his running more seriously from then on.

Using training methods he had been taught as a child, Ted started working out six days each week, logging up to 160 kilometres per week with long runs, easy runs for recovery, and speed training to increase his pain tolerance. In Ethiopia, no one runs for exercise as is common in Canada. The lifestyle there, which includes plenty of daily walking, is conducive to fitness.

Ted's increased training had a remarkable effect on his performance in a very short period of time. In the Moose Jaw race, he had run 10 kilometres in 46 minutes, which is a seven-and-a-half-minute mile. That is not bad for most people, but Ted knew he should have been able to go much faster than that. "When I was younger, I was running about a five-minute mile for that distance. That was world-class level."

By August 1985, barely three months after his dismal first showing in Moose Jaw, Ted competed in the Regina Downtown Dash. His time improved by eight minutes. That much of a reduction in such a short period surprised everyone. He started getting attention from the other runners, who asked questions about his training methods.

Each time, Ted's answer was the same. Hard work is essential.

"If you're willing to do the work, your body will respond. You have to have the desire and willingness to train outside your comfort zone. If you train slow, your body will run slow. The greater the demand you place on your body within its limits, the more your body will adapt and strengthen and become more efficient. This training will help you during the race to sustain your speed for a prolonged time. You have to endure the pain threshold."

Ted continued to improve in races. In September, he went to Saskatoon with his new group of friends. He ran 10 kilometres in 37 minutes, another improvement. The race season then came to an end for the year and Ted decided to join the track club for a more structured training environment.

Although his running partners tried to talk him into staying with them as a recreational runner, Ted turned down their requests. As usual, he had made a decision and he had to act on it. Ted joined the Regina Wheat City Kinsmen Track and Field Club in the fall of 1985 and began to train alongside the higher-calibre athletes there.

By this point, Ted was taking Administration classes at the University of Regina, having made that decision when the photo lab closed. He spent much of his time away from school either running, training for races or working at various part-time jobs.

He worked the night shift operating a mail-processing machine and was a bouncer at the casino on the Exhibition grounds, mostly checking for proper photo identification to ensure underage individuals didn't enter. He was also called when the Regina Exhibition Association needed workers for specific events such as the annual week-long Buffalo Days fair or various banquets.

Ted remembers being asked to pour wine at one event and then being quickly pulled off that job. "I spilled wine on one of the ladies and she freaked out. And I never had that job again. I went back to being a bouncer, and they let me pour beer from a keg sometimes. I was good at that one. That was easy."

With the home of the Canadian Football League's Saskatchewan Roughriders just down the street from the Exhibition grounds at Taylor Field, Ted was often mistaken for one of the players. When inebriated customers would ask him if he was a 'Rider, Ted would smile and mischievously reply: 'Yes, I'm a wide receiver.'

Ted saw a significant improvement in his running results the first winter he trained with the Wheat City track club. In May 1986, he travelled with some of the track club members to Yorkton, northeast of Regina, to participate in the Go 4 Sports 10-kilometre race.

Up until that point, the province's high-calibre runners had been beating him. The year before, when he was running 38 minutes, they were running 33 or 32 minutes. "That's almost a mile ahead of me," explains Ted, who didn't plan on anything more than just beating his own time, which is what most runners attempt to do in each race.

The race was two times around a five-kilometre loop. After the first loop, Ted was pleased to see he was still keeping up with the front runners. In 10K races, the most crucial part of the race is from six kilometres to the end. That's the point where runners are the most weary and those in behind the leader often step it up to win.

At the 6K mark in this race, Ted sensed that the front runners were nervous. He saw that their breathing patterns were rough and he used that moment to surge forward. With about two kilometres to go, he looked back to see the other runners were about 50 metres behind him. He was determined not to lose his lead and he pressed hard for the next two kilometres to gain about a 30-second advantage on them and win the race.

It was the first race that Ted won on Canadian soil and it was the first significant race he won since his high school championship in Ethiopia in 1972. The other top-place finishers were in their early 20s. Ted was 31.

Winning the 1986 Yorkton event opened a new chapter in Ted's life. He now had a renewed sense of achievement and the confidence to pursue some of the running goals he had lost because of the war.

"I had never really forgotten my unfinished business of running. I now felt I had gotten control of my life. After that, the things I worried about in Canada like social barriers, fitting in with the Canadian culture and learning new life skills, started to come easier."

Ted continued on the running circuit in Saskatchewan and participated in most races, including the Timex Road Racing series for the rest of that season. Every weekend, he'd travel and compete. He continued to excel in the sport he loves.

* * *

In September 1986, on his own birthday, the most significant event of Ted's adult life occurred. He became a father. For about two years, Ted had dated a woman who lived in the same neighbourhood as he did. When she became pregnant, Ted looked forward to becoming a parent. His eyes light up and his face glows with the memory of the first time he held his newborn son, Adam.

"Holding him in my arms gave me a rush of joy. Tears came to my eyes and it was an incredible feeling even to be alive. Adam's arrival gave me a positive perspective about the future. Everything had changed. Now I had my own family. I had a purpose to live again."

Ted and Adam's mother shared a rocky relationship for about five years, going their separate ways in 1989. Adam continued to live with his mother but saw his father regularly. His parents shared responsibility for raising him and Ted has remained an active part of his son's life.

Ted learned a lot from his former partner. He notes she is a hard worker, which encouraged him to continue to work hard as well. She also had some challenges in her background and overcame them.

Ted has dated other women over the years but has never married. He knows that his past came back to haunt him in some of his early relationships. He didn't have any sense of trust because he was forced to suppress his feelings. "You can have a relationship but still feel empty. When I came to this strange country, there were probably a lot of people who cared about me, but in those early years I was so lonely. Even with a girlfriend, I was empty inside."

War and destitution had left many emotional scars. After such cruel treatment, shutting down emotionally was a way for Ted to cope. A key way for Ted to heal has been in talking about it. He has begun to open himself up to others, allowing himself to find some peace within.

Chapter Nine

Building Momentum

As Ted spent more time and energy on training and running, his race results improved. He began to dominate in races all over the province, almost always finishing in the top few positions. He also started attracting attention province-wide.

He began to field requests for his advice, and individuals asked if they could train with him to learn better techniques. Some runners were mildly interested in his background and skills. Others quickly became lifelong friends and teased him about his idiosyncrasies.

Darren Burrows, a runner who is an accountant in Calgary, first saw Ted in 1985 when Burrows was in Grade 9 and running in a race held in Lumsden, a town just northwest of Regina. "It was a 10K race. Ted and another friend of his were at this race. It was odd because he was the first black guy you'd see out at these road races. I ended up beating him by quite a bit," recalls Burrows.

"I remember another time when I was driving with my friends at lunch hour. It was the middle of winter and we looked over and here's this guy driving along and he's got his Skidoo mitts on, the ones that go up to your elbows almost, and he's got a hood pulled up with a toque and a mask on, inside of his car! We're all sitting there, high schoolers, laughing at this guy and wondering how he could be so cold. And then I looked and saw it was Ted, so we were honking the horn, and he gave us this big smile and wave. That would have been a couple of years after he got here. He never enjoyed the cold," laughs Burrows.

Jason Warick, another runner who is a journalist in Saskatoon, agrees that Ted is sometimes unintentionally entertaining in the wintertime. "He always wears way more clothes than we do when we go out for winter runs. If it's five degrees below zero, we'll be wearing a light toque, some very light gloves and maybe a thin jacket. Ted will be bundled up in a parka and a huge balaclava and those big leather mitts that go up to your elbows, and all you can see are his eyes. It's just funny."

Burrows recalls seeing another side of Ted when he was welcomed into Ted's apartment for a glass of orange juice after a run. The lack of food in Ted's kitchen was mind-boggling. "He'd have orange juice, a couple cans of spaghetti sauce, some pasta noodles on the shelf and maybe two bananas," recalls Burrows. "Coming from a home where my parents provided everything, seeing how hard he had to work to make things go was a good eye opener for me."

Burrows and his young track club friends quickly welcomed Ted into their fold and teased him about his simple diet. "We'd always bug him: 'What are you having for lunch today? Spaghetti? What about your next meal? Oh, yeah, probably spaghetti, hey?' It's been kind of funny to watch Ted evolve into being almost Canadianized. He would know we were teasing him but he didn't know how to say the right thing back all the time. To watch him evolve and pick up our sense of humour and sarcasm as the years went by has been great."

Ted's adjustment to Canadian humour was also evident the first time he introduced Carl and Fay Burton to one of his friends after a race in Saskatoon. It was in 1986. "He came over to us with his friend and this friend was as blond as Ted is dark," recalls Fay. "Ted said: 'I would like you to meet my mom and dad,' and this friend looked at us and at Ted and said: 'Oh, sure, Ted.' Because here's Ted, mahogany colour, and Carl and I are white," Fay laughs.

"It was a chuckle for us and for Ted, too, when he realized what he said. In Amharic, the language he speaks, 'mom and dad' doesn't have the same connotation as 'mom and dad' does over here. It would be no different than if he called us Carl and Fay."

Fay looks back fondly on moments such as those. "Ted was already striving ahead. He kept making that ultimate effort to better himself. I'm proud to call him my proxy son."

Warick and Burrows have been both friend and foe to Ted for many years. Literally. While they have shared many laughs and deep conversations, they have also challenged each other on the racing circuit.

"Ted's incredibly fast but he has one gear," laughs Warick. "He runs the same pace whether it's a marathon or 10K or 1500 metres."

Ted has specifically trained himself to run the same speed for 20K. Endurance has always been his strong point.

Since Warick's first glimpse of Ted when Warick was a 10-year-old watching "these fast guys" go up to the podium to get their awards for the Regina Downtown Dash, he has aspired to be like Ted and those other winners. "Once I got to be a really good runner, I always thought: 'Maybe I'll beat Ted this year,' but he always found a way to beat me. I think I got second four years in a row." Warick finally won the Downtown Dash after Ted retired from competitive racing.

Hearing Ted's story has helped Warick appreciate more of the world around him and the advantages that come with living in North America. "We in Saskatchewan can try to accomplish things and we have a lot of support for whatever it is we want to achieve, whether it's music, art or sports. There are really no major obstacles. If we want to pursue something, we can do it because we're a free society and we have all these opportunities and all this wealth in our society," Warick believes.

"Ted struggled for a while and then he found his groove. That's why I see him as a bit of a mentor and a hero. Whenever I think of the goals that I have, if I get lazy or I think that something's too difficult, I just think of what he's had to overcome and then I don't complain too much about my own situation."

For Ted, running has provided him with a level playing field to succeed in Canada. "When you line up to begin a race, it's a fair start for everybody," Ted believes.

* * *

One day in 1987, while Ted was changing his clothes at the Regina YMCA after a noon-hour run, a representative for Saucony, a running shoes and clothing manufacturing company, approached him and offered him a sponsorship deal. In exchange for wearing Saucony gear during running events, Ted would be provided with free Saucony running shoes and clothing. Ted gladly accepted the offer.

Shoes lose support for long distance running after 800 kilometres. Ted was going through shoes every few weeks at that time. A good pair of shoes in 2006 could cost about $130 CDN and a tracksuit with jacket and pants about $250. The Spandex tracksuit Ted wears in the winter months is worth about $200.

"Their support came when I needed it most. They believed in me and I'm grateful for that."

In 1988, Ted became much more visible to the Regina public after the local newspaper profiled him twice within a month. With headlines like: 'Jaleta Isn't Running For His Life Anymore' and 'Jaleta's Legs Let Him Escape Ethiopia,' who wouldn't take notice? The articles by *Regina Leader-Post* sports writer Les Donison exposed readers to some of Ted's background and raised his profile considerably as a talented local runner. The articles also detailed how Ted won the Fort Qu'Appelle/Echo Lake road race that weekend for the first time.

Ted told the newspaper how he had quit smoking to take up running again and how running made him happy and more fulfilled. "Days when I don't run, I feel guilty," he said. "I'd like to compete for the rest of my life, at least until I'm about 40 or 45. It's hard to quit once you've been hooked."[20]

* * *

In recalling his racing progress in Saskatchewan, Ted says: "By 1989, I was mostly untouchable in the province. Winning, winning, winning."

This is not a statement from an egotistical athlete. In Ted Jaleta's case, it is simply the truth.

One of the reasons he won all those races – and a reason Ted has done so well in so many other areas of his life – can be summed up in one word. Discipline.

Darren Burrows started training full-time with Ted in the fall of 1987. He recalls how difficult it was to keep up with the 33-year-old's running schedule. "Ted made sure the runs we were doing on Sunday mornings were at about 8 o'clock. We would go out for 27 kilometres. He was very disciplined with getting in all his workouts, which was tough for me, a guy 17 years old."

The two men not only attended university at the same time but also trained together and raced against each other in events all over Canada until 1998 when Burrows moved to Calgary. "I basically have the notoriety of losing to Ted for 10 years straight on the road, getting second place," laughs Burrows. "I could beat him no problem in 1500 to 5000 metres on the track. I couldn't beat him at anything after 5000. I came close a few times, but he always had enough to hold me off."

Ted's ability to prioritize running in his daily life is what has contributed to his success as a runner, according to Burrows. "He had to do that to compete at an elite level. It has always had to be a priority to get the training done, whether that meant going to bed early on a Saturday night or something else."

Burrows tells about a particular evening in Ottawa after the national championships. "In some cases, we'd go out to party the night after the race. One time, we were actually in the middle of a song on the dance floor and Ted checked his watch. It was 12:30 on the nose and he'd obviously told himself, because he's so disciplined, that: 'At 12:30, I'm leaving.' So as we're standing out there in the middle of the floor dancing, Ted looked at his watch and turned and said: 'I have to go now.' And he walked off the dance floor and left me with the two girls. He caught a cab and headed back to the motel and went to bed," adds Burrows with a laugh.

Ted doesn't much care to slot people into age categories or compartments either. "We are different ages. It doesn't matter to Ted," says Warick. "He's got friends that are all over the map culturally and age-wise. He realizes life is short and these superficial things don't matter."

Warick's relationship with Ted grew in the mid 1990s while he attended the University of Regina as well. Ted is "young-hearted," says Warick, who admits he finds that surprising. "I would have expected somebody that's been through the hell that he has been through to come out on the other end with a really jaded view and be really bitter, but he's not. He's really curious about everything. Ted looks at everything with fresh eyes."

Ted would also be the last person to consider himself special or blessed. "He doesn't have any romantic notions about why he has been allowed to survive and get out of that situation in Ethiopia," Warick adds. "Some people live and some people die and that's the way life goes. That is not to say Ted doesn't feel anything for the people that haven't made it. He feels a connection to the people he's seen die or those who have not been able to escape the prison where he was, and I think it weighs on him. I think that motivates him to do whatever he's doing in his life in their name. He wants to help other people as a way of honouring those who would have taken his place if he hadn't made it out of there."

Ted calls himself decisive but Warick has another word for it. "Sometimes I think he's stubborn. He's very set in certain things. He's wide-eyed and open-minded in most things in life, but he's accomplished a lot of things because his resolve is pretty firm. When we're doing workouts, if he's got it in his mind he has to run six miles at this pace, he'll do it even if he's got a cold or even if it's a snowstorm. Even when we go out for supper, if he's got some place in mind, he'll advocate for it," Warick laughs.

Ted is always analyzing situations and the people around him. He quickly reads other people's body language and knows before most others in the room if the person he's facing is nervous, tired, confused or feeling something else. It is part of the reason he survived the war and detention. He can tell in an instant what is really going on inside the heads of those around him.

In the workplace, as in most of his everyday life, Ted does not hold back his comments or suggestions. He seldom criticizes and he participates in discussions at work, asking questions about decisions that don't make sense to him. "I express my opinions, but not in a negative way. I am a team player and I want to improve communication and create more understanding between workers and supervisors."

Ted appreciates the freedom to speak his mind in Canada and takes advantage of opportunities he has to say something that might improve the world around him. In fact, he has not been able to hold back his thoughts since he overcame his fear of speaking up while sitting on that dirt floor in elementary school decades ago. He knows that he needs to express his thoughts to be who he is meant to be. He cannot stay quiet. "If I do that, it will kill me inside."

* * *

By the end of the 1980s, Ted had picked up steam to become a well-known road racer locally, provincially and nationally. He was getting invitations to races in other provinces and had many interesting experiences from those events.

Ted ran in an invitational race in Vancouver, British Columbia, in July 1989. He planned to relax after that race and have a short vacation. Those plans changed after he walked into a convenience store and saw an entry form for another race later that week, the C Fox Trot 8K.

The traditional rest period after a race is one day for each mile run.

Ted should have stayed away from running for the remainder of his vacation, but he decided it would be fun to compete in the C Fox Trot, so he filled out the entry form.

At the start line, Ted listened to the local high-calibre runners talk to each other about which one of them would win the race. Ted thought he might surprise them with his abilities, but he wasn't sure. He did not know their capabilities and they did not know who he was either. They were all at a disadvantage in not knowing how to exploit each other's weaknesses during the race. Ted decided the best he could do was run with the leaders for a while and see what developed.

At the four-kilometre mark of the 8K race, Ted was still with the front runners and they were glancing at him in wonder. By the six-kilometre mark, the front pack had become smaller and Ted was keeping up with the young leader, who tried to break away heading up a hill. Ted simply stayed with him, to the other runner's surprise.

Ted often talks about the "hill workout" training he had as a child in Ethiopia when, for fun on the way to school, the boys would race each other. Ted often used his endurance to run quickly to the top of a hill where he waited for the other children to reach him. Before the others could catch their breath at the top, Ted would be off again, running ahead of them. He knew the other boys could run faster than he could in the final sprint, so his goal was always to get a head start so they would never catch him.

Ted says his strategy for running across the hills of Ethiopia as a child can be applied to everyday life. "We were kids just trying to have fun and compete with each other, but in the real world we can learn from our achievements. If we use our strengths to reach our goals and create strategies to win, we are empowered for success."

The young man leading the Vancouver race that day had never seen anything like this hill-climbing Ted Jaleta before. After he and Ted reached the top of the hill, they glanced back and saw that they were definitely in the lead.

"We had already gained 50 metres on the other two people that were with us and I could sense he was hurting," Ted says about the leader. "When we got to the flat course, I used my monster surge and I broke away. I won by 30 seconds." Ted also set a course record that day.

A wide grin covers Ted's face as he talks about the satisfaction of winning that race. "It was memorable because I was the unexpected winner and they could not believe this could happen to them."

When running at the front of a race with strong competitors, Ted has often said he prefers to follow rather than lead. "When you are leading, it is a lot of effort to set the pace. I prefer to follow until the leaders get tired. That's when I use my strength and endurance to try to win the race."

It's not often that Ted looks back to see what is behind him. "When I do glance behind me, I don't like to be noticed. The other racers might think that is a weakness, showing that I am getting tired, and they might get encouraged. I don't like to show my weaknesses when I'm competing," he says with a smile.

All of a sudden, Ted stares at his feet and wonders aloud about his own weaknesses. His expression changes from one of pure joy to one of deep concentration. "Do you have a darkest fear?" he asks rhetorically.

For the briefest of moments, he opens his soul to allow a glimpse into the rawest of his wounds.

"Mine is fear of failure. Failure, and to starve again."

These are the deep-seated reasons behind Ted's drive. They are the reasons for his discipline, his determination and his winning.

* * *

Ted's routine in preparing for a race has remained relatively the same for 20 years. He alternates workouts and gradually increases the distance he runs and the intensity of his training to improve his endurance.

On Sundays, he'll have his longest run of the week, at about two hours duration for 25 to 30K. The next day, he'll have an easy recovery run and on Tuesdays, he'll do easy runs in the morning and speed sessions in the evening. Wednesday's schedule includes another easy recovery run and Thursday is the day to run 'intervals,' repeating the same distance to increase speed. Friday is a day off from running and Saturday is marked for speed and endurance workouts, possibly climbing hills.

Ted also does some weightlifting, but only enough to increase core stability. "I like to stay lean and slim," he says. "Having more muscle creates body mass, which will slow a runner down. Any exercise helps improve muscle strength."

If Ted is competing in a race in Regina, he will arrive at the course at least an hour before the start time. If the race is far outside the city or outside the province, he will arrive at least a day beforehand to allow himself time to be physically ready to compete. He'll check out the course before the race, either on the entry form or in person once he reaches the location. In some bigger races, organizers lead tours of the race course the day before the event.

On the morning of a race, Ted will wake at 6 a.m. and go for a 20-minute run. He'll then go back to either his apartment or the place where he's staying and do some stretches. He'll drink a glass of water or orange juice and eat a piece of toast. That will be followed by a half a cup of coffee. Black. No sugar.

Wearing long pants and a long-sleeved jacket to keep his muscles warm, even in the summertime, Ted will arrive at the course about an hour before the race is scheduled to begin. About 45 minutes before the start, Ted does an easy jog for 20 to 30 minutes.

Only a few others are jogging at this point prior to the race and it would be unusual to see another runner in Saskatchewan with the same concentration etched on his or her face. The intensity is at a different level with Ted. Even during his easy warm-up jogs, it is difficult for others to break Ted's concentration.

Ted suggests that all runners should warm up before the race. Just as an automobile needs to be warmed up in the wintertime to work better, a runner's legs will generate more speed if they are warm. Like an automobile, an athlete's legs need a longer warm-up period in colder temperatures.

After his easy jog, Ted stretches and then runs sprints for about 10 minutes to prepare his legs for what is about to happen next. At a typical race, he leaves his sweats on until five minutes before the start. Again, this helps to keep his muscles warm. He then puts on his singlet, a sleeveless shirt, and pins his runner's race number to the front of it. He heads to the starting line, moving his legs constantly until the race begins.

To the uninitiated eye, this last-minute change of clothing is disarming. But to Ted, it is a routine that has been finely tuned for optimum performance over many races and many years. When the race begins, Ted is more than ready.

Placing in the top three positions in a local or provincial race usually earns the runner a trophy or ribbon and a small cash award. Local race entry fees range from $20 to $50 per race and the cash award for the top finishers is generally at least double the entry fee. Ted's results since the late 1980s almost always covered his expenses for races within and outside the province. Entry fees to national races are higher, at around $100, but these are subsidized by the provincial running associations.

The cash awards that go with winning helped spur Ted on to victory in his early years of running when he struggled to pay his own bills while in university and help financially to raise his son. For many years, Ted has also sent money to Ethiopia to help family members with university or college expenses.

In 1990, Ted was the provincial Timex Road Race Series champion for accumulating the most points for each of his finishes. Over the next few years, he made the provincial team to go to the nationals or other events, but occasionally turned down racing opportunities to attend events such as his son's birthday parties or piano recitals. "Being with Adam was more important to me than running."

However, in December 1990, Ted decided he had to leave Adam for a while to take one last shot at his own dream.

He travelled to Dallas, Texas, to see if, at age 36, he could achieve a qualifying time for the marathon in the 1992 Olympic Games in Barcelona. Ted phoned to talk to Adam often during the six months that he was away, but he lived with the guilt of leaving his child behind so he could pursue his own passion.

Ted's training period in warm weather went well and he returned to Canada with renewed determination to further condition himself for a marathon qualifying time.

In May 1991, Ted ran two races in the Rocky Mountains of Alberta that have stayed in his memory for different reasons.

The Jasper-Banff relay has about 12 runners on a team, each racing a distance of up to 20 kilometres and then passing a baton to the next person on the team for the next leg of the race. Ted ran the first section of this race for his team, against some high-calibre athletes from Japan. He won his leg of the race with a photo finish.

Ted's team didn't win the entire relay but it was an incredible feeling nonetheless to win his leg against runners who were usually faster than him. "It was challenging and satisfying. When racing against someone as good as you are, it makes you dig to bring the best out of yourself. I would rather run a fast time and lose than run a slow time and win. That is more fulfilling."

He also recalls a 10K run a few weeks later in the town of Banff, which is in the midst of a national park full of evergreen trees, foothills, mountains and the occasional elk or deer that might wander on to the course. That race was notable because of the strong flashbacks he had of his homeland.

"During races, there are times when I drift away to revisit my past. I am aware of where I'm going when I'm running. At the same time, I am recalling events from my childhood, like running through the mountains and playing with my sisters and brothers. I also see myself when I was escaping from the detention centre and my life in exile," Ted explains.

"Near the end of that Banff race, I woke up from the dream and realized I was in Canada and I was running for glory. When I crossed that finish line, it was kind of a strange feeling. I was grateful to even be alive. I never thought I would survive that turmoil. And I was running here, on top of the world, and winning the race. It was just incredible. I was full of mixed emotions."

Places that look like his home in the hills of Ethiopia, such as Banff and Saskatchewan's Qu'Appelle Valley, are where Ted is particularly prone to flashbacks. These episodes in the midst of races have lasted as long as 30 minutes, with his mind reliving scenes of his life and helping him to cope with the experiences he has had. "In a way, it masks the pain and fatigue I feel when I run."

Ted usually comes out of his daydreams at the halfway points, where the runners are given their split times for sections of the race, or at corners where spectators are gathered to cheer on the athletes.

Marion Craig, a high-calibre runner who has also coached with Ted, explains that each athlete responds differently to the pressure of long distance running. "Some people associate directly with what they're doing. Others disconnect. The intensity of what you're doing is extremely focused. The highest-calibre runners may zone out for a while but they are still very much in touch with where they are, who is breathing down their neck, what their split times are and what they need to do to win the race," she says.

"The naturally-talented elite athletes like Ted come up with this ability to move out of their comfort zone and deal with the excruciating pain of running long distances. We all ask ourselves: 'How do I get out of my comfort zone?' Some athletes have it naturally. Ted Jaleta is one of those."

In June 1991, Ted returned to Regina after the Banff race and was playing soccer in a field with his then-six-year-old son. As often happens on the flat prairie surrounding Regina, there are colonies of gophers, or Richardson's ground squirrels as they are more accurately called, that make their homes in the ground and leave large holes on the surface as entries to their tunnels. While playing soccer that day, Ted stepped in a gopher hole and severely twisted an ankle, ending his hopes of qualifying for the 1992 Olympics.

He lost all conditioning, but that wasn't the only reason that Ted did not follow through on his quest for the Olympic Games that year. Adam was still young and Ted wasn't focused enough on racing. He struggled between being a parent and competitive running. His son came first.

The twisted ankle meant the end of another dream, but it wasn't the end of the world for Ted.

"Going to the Olympics is not everything," he says. Although it is a recognition of an athlete's achievements, Ted believes he would not likely have won at that point anyway. His prime racing years were gone. He had lost some of his speed and was older than most of the other athletes. "Olympians are full-time runners. I was not. For me, it would have been great to go only to say I had been there."

Ted's last shot at the Olympics had disappeared, but he started on a different path that year. He was hired as a federal government employee of the Canada Revenue Agency.

"I was recovering from my injury and I saw an employment notice. The guy that was working in the mailroom got hit by a bus and they had to replace him."

Ted laughs at the odd circumstances that led to him getting hired with the Revenue Agency. He quickly adds that the other man was only off work temporarily and returned to the job a few months later after recovering from his injuries. Ted's new job led him into a fulfilling career with the federal civil service and provided him with more opportunities to help people.

Since 1991, he has worked in the mailroom, in procurement, in income tax client services and in accounts receivable for the Canadian equivalent of the Internal Revenue Service. He has enjoyed his job and the agency has enjoyed having him as an employee.

Debbie Johnson, a Canada Revenue Agency co-worker, is impressed by Ted's success in Canada. "When he came here, he couldn't speak the language. The only thing he knew that we ate was Corn Flakes and chicken. He's one of those people who achieves great things quietly. He doesn't come on in a grand fashion when you meet him. He just works very steadily and accomplishes great things. It's a tribute to his tenacity and perseverance."

Johnson notes that Ted worked his way up from the mailroom to the inquiries unit and had to learn English to a far greater degree than other immigrants do to deal with their clients. "He's worked so hard, both for us and for all Canadians, and he's certainly helped to put us on the map: us as his employer, we in Regina, we in Saskatchewan."

Ted believes his past has helped him learn how to deal with people in despair. A technical tax consultant needs patience to help clients understand complex tax issues and Ted can easily relate to the difficulties that some of his clients face. "This helps me perform my job better. I can also help them realize how lucky they are as citizens of this wonderful country and how bad things can be elsewhere."

Dave Marshall, assistant director of revenue collections with Canada Revenue Agency in Regina, recalls an incident when a client came in to complain about how she was unable to repay her unwarranted tax refund. She was frustrated and flustered and said to Ted: 'You don't know what it's like to be poor.' Then the woman's cell phone went off in her purse."

Ted told the woman about his life in the refugee camp, where he sometimes had only one bowl of porridge a day. "In this country, it is not an issue of dying from starvation because of our social safety nets. Where I came from, assistance like that is unheard of," he says. Ted's conversation with the woman helped her re-evaluate her priorities and led to her paying off her outstanding bills.

"Ted's a bit of an ambassador for our agency here," adds Marshall. "He has a very positive attitude. He lives one day at a time, makes the best out of the day and doesn't look back and dwell on negative things. He has an attitude of gratitude."

* * *

On the running front, Ted continued to win race after race locally. His talents were obvious to everyone, even young Adam. In 1992, while at a race with his father one weekend, six-year-old Adam couldn't believe his eyes when Ted finished second.

Adam walked up to his father and bluntly stated: "That other guy must have cheated! My dad can't lose!"

The thought of his son's confidence in him that day has helped Ted through many dark moments in his life since. One of those came in 1993, when he received a letter telling him that his beloved youngest sister Sadate had died from breast cancer.

When the letter arrived, Ted had just tucked it in his pocket to read later during a break at work. He assumed it would contain the usual greetings from his family, and he was looking forward to catching up on their latest news. Instead, he felt the tears trickle down his face. "I could not believe what I was reading."

He walked quickly to the men's washroom to read the rest of the letter and stayed there, in a washroom cubicle, for about half an hour, trying desperately to come to grips with the news. A co-worker came by and asked him if he was OK. "I did not tell them. I said I was not feeling well and I had to go home." Ted didn't think anyone would understand his pain.

He had not seen Sadate since he had said goodbye to her the night he left Ethiopia. Now he would never see her again.

Ted is eternally grateful for his sister's kindness when he was in hiding in Ethiopia. "When I received the news of her death, I felt part of me died with her."

When he got home, he phoned his girlfriend. They had been dating for about four years and her support helped him through the pain. "We boys were raised not to cry, not to show emotions. That's a universal culture. Sometimes, you cannot control your emotions."

A year later, another letter arrived with bad news from Ethiopia. Ted's mother had died. He was devastated.

When he got this news, Ted was alone at home. He phoned work the next day and told them what happened. He took a week off work to mourn and was pleasantly surprised when an envelope arrived the next day from his co-workers. It was a sympathy card with a gift of money they had collected for Ted to send to Ethiopia to help his family with funeral expenses.

Ted couldn't go to Ethiopia for either of the funerals. It was not safe. The Mengistu government had only toppled in 1992 with the collapse of the Soviet Union and the country's political climate was still unstable. So he stayed in Canada and mourned the loss of his loved ones, mostly by himself.

"A lot of the stuff with his African past, the pain he went through, he dealt with on his own," says Darren Burrows. "It was kind of weird. His mother had passed away but he didn't mention it for quite some time. I think that was really tough on him."

Ted admits that, for good or bad, his past has affected him. "I have a tendency not to rely on other people. I deal with it myself."

* * *

Ted, as a runner, was getting better with age, often winning against runners who were 10 to 20 years younger. "Competitive training was really not expected in Ethiopia until our later teens," he explains. "This is where we differ from Canadian culture. Intense training did not happen until about 16 years of age, therefore we were able to withstand the demands of high-calibre competitive running for many years, with less burnout than we typically see here in Canada."

Ted won the Echo Lake road race for the seventh consecutive time in 1994 and the next year, finished first place overall in the men's division at the annual 10K Sweetheart Run in Regina. He stated again that he was a long way from retirement as a runner and that more people should stay in shape by exercising. "People say they don't have the time, but you can make the time if you have the desire to do it. We waste a couple of hours sitting in front of the TV every day," he said.[21]

For Ted, racing is fun. "A race is just a half hour of going fast. Every time I train, I get more knowledge in every aspect of running. It's one of the things that makes me most happy in life."[22] Ted has always put considerable energy into training for a race, so running the race is the fulfilling part of the process for him.

In 1995, Ted was again proclaimed 'the premier road racer in the province' by the local newspaper. He had won the annual Sweetheart Run in Regina again and had finished first in another 10K road race in the southeastern Saskatchewan city of Estevan with a course record time of 30:23 minutes. As incredible as it sounds, at age 41, Ted was running the same time he ran in Ethiopia when he was 17.

"This is probably the best shape that Ted's been in," Darren Burrows told the newspaper. "Sure, other people put in lots of miles but I don't think they put in the interval training that Ted does. You don't see that intensity. We've been training together over the winter but not all the time. To beat Ted, you have to be consistent."[23]

Ted was indeed becoming a phenomenon in long distance running in Saskatchewan, and more was yet to come.

Over 14 years, between August 23, 1986 and June 25, 2000, Ted Jaleta ran in 52 community level races in Saskatchewan ranging in length from 5K to half marathons. He finished first in 43 of those races and won the second-place award five times. It is an amazing accomplishment that will not likely be seen again in Saskatchewan any time soon.

A typical example of Ted's finishes in Saskatchewan races involves two young women who have run in the Regina Downtown Dash 5K event for the last number of years. They routinely visit with Ted at the beginning of every race and joke with him. "Their goal is always to finish 5K before I get to the finish line of the 10K. A few times I almost caught them on the wire," Ted smiles.

Few would denigrate Ted's athletic abilities and Ted himself would never diminish the other runners' efforts.

"I've been there. I know that feeling," he says of being far behind the leading runner. "I'm sure they can run faster," he says with a grin. All it would take is a little coaching and more practice. But Ted quickly adds that his style of training and running is not for everyone.

"It doesn't matter how you finish. Run against yourself. Run for fitness," he urges.

CHAPTER TEN

STRIVING FOR EXCELLENCE

As Ted's wins in Saskatchewan increased, he decided to challenge himself further by testing his skills on the international Masters circuit, for runners age 40 and older, in the United States. He made a few phone calls and, in May 1996, was invited to compete in the annual Bolder Boulder, a 6.2 mile race in Colorado held on Memorial Day that drew more than 37,000 entrants. Ted had run with about 5,000 other people in a race in Dallas when he was training in the U.S. in 1991, but this was a whole new experience.

Ted enjoyed his view of the Rocky Mountains on the 45-minute ride from the Denver airport northwest to the city of Boulder. He checked into his hotel, which was within walking distance of the race starting line, and was pleased to find that several other runners invited to the race were from Kenya.

"That was fun to hang around with them," recalls Ted. His roommate was Joseph Nzau, a former Olympian. Nzau was 44 years old at the time and has been referred to as the 'pioneer of Kenyan running.' At the 1984 Summer Olympics, he placed sixth in the marathon and 10th in the 10K race for his native Kenya.[24]

The invited athletes were taken on a bus tour of the course that runs through downtown Boulder. Ted thought it was exciting to see where the race started and ended. The city itself has an elevation of 5,300 feet. This would be Ted's first race at a high altitude since leaving Ethiopia. He was curious to see how he would place.

At the hotel, the invited runners enjoyed a hospitality room that had a constant supply of food and beverages, plus free massages. Volunteers offered maps of the area or transportation if requested. Ted's hotel room had been paid for by the race organizers and he felt like royalty. It was an excellent introduction to the international Masters circuit.

On race day, Ted lined up at the front of the start line with the other high-calibre invited runners and waited for the signal to go. Behind him were thousands of other runners, joggers, walkers and wheelchair racers ready to take on what is one of the largest road races in the world.[25]

Before Ted got to Boulder, he knew what to expect of his competitors in that race. He knew their expected times and his own abilities. "I knew I was a contender."

He was excited to compete at that level and not nervous at all. Ted is never nervous before a race. He had done the work to get there. Now all he had to do was run, which he did.

Ted ran the race according to his plan and was the winner of the men's Masters division, beating Masters competitors from all over the world. "That was my debut in the U.S.," says Ted proudly. "Winning was unexpected. Right away, everybody knew who I was."

Well, almost everyone.

At the finish line, the local media announced the favoured American runner as the winner of the Masters category instead of Ted's name, likely because they were unfamiliar with this newcomer. Also, Ted is often mistaken for being 10 to 20 years younger than his real age. The announcers quickly corrected their error and Ted was escorted to the cubicle where the media waited to interview the winners on live TV.

"I didn't think it was a big deal at the time, but it was great," recalls Ted. At the awards ceremony afterwards, he was asked for his autograph and was pleased to oblige.

After the race, he was driven to the airport and the organizers made good on their earlier promise of paying for not only his hotel and food, but reimbursing him for his airfare if he won. Ted recalls winning about $1,000 USD for his placing that day. It was the largest amount he had ever won and, for the first time, more than covered his expenses.

In August 1996, Ted finished third in the Masters category at a 7.1-mile race in Falmouth, Massachusetts. In September, he placed second in Masters in the Chicago Half Marathon. He announced to the Regina media in October 1996 that he would be cutting back on his local running in the coming year by 90% to focus on the Masters road racing circuit in the United States.

"Most people who are finishing ahead of me in the international races are from Mexico, Russia or Poland. There usually aren't any North Americans ahead of me," he said.[26] Ted was also seeing places that he couldn't afford to go to on his own.

* * *

In Ted's running career, 1997 was definitely his best year. On the international circuit, he competed in nine races in Florida, Nevada, Alabama, Louisiana, Washington, Colorado, New York, Massachusetts and Michigan. He finished second in the Masters division in seven of those races, third once and fourth once, racing in all kinds of climates on many different terrains.

On February 9, 1997, in the desert city of Las Vegas, he came in second in the 21.1-kilometre Las Vegas International Half-Marathon and set the Canadian Half-Marathon Masters record for men age 40 and over with a time of 65:54 minutes. That record still stands.

In most of his international races that year, Ted finished behind one of the world's greatest runners, former Olympian Steve Jones of Great Britain. "I was pleased at the time to do so well against a runner of his calibre," says Ted, who was also a little star-struck by Jones. Ted asked for his autograph and had his photo taken with Jones after one of the races.

Ted's finishes in these international races was all the more remarkable because of the difference in his training techniques and those of his competitors. While Ted was juggling work and training, the people running against him were full-time runners with full sponsorships, which gave them an advantage to produce better results. The other runners also did not have to train in the harsh winters in Canada. They went to Mexico or the southern U.S. or other warmer places to train. Ted did not have that luxury.

In 1997, Ted flew about 135,000 kilometres on Northwest Airlines. He was gone almost every weekend to race in either the United States or Canada and almost always came back a winner. He finished second overall among men from all the age categories in the Banff Citizen 10K run in June 1997 and was the overall men's winner in the Calgary Herald 10K in September. In 1997, Ted was also the Canadian Masters 10K Road Race Champion for the third consecutive year.

The trips to the U.S. did not cost Ted anything financially. His expenses were paid and by finishing in the top five on the international Masters circuit, Ted also earned between $500 and $1,500 USD a race. The top 15 overall finishers also received a cash prize, so Ted usually won money for finishing in the top five in his Masters age group and for being an overall top finisher as well. He didn't get rich from these races and he often used holiday time to go to the competitions. His rewards came mostly in the form of satisfaction, knowing that his training was paying off and his talents were being recognized.

Ted competed in the 10-mile Crim Festival of Races in Flint, Michigan, in August that year and was applauded there for more than just his placing in the race. A newspaper clipping from a Michigan paper talked about 29-year-old Brahim Lahlifi of Morocco who was the winner, "beating nine Kenyans to the downtown finish line. A special thanks should go to Masters runner Ted Jaleta from Canada. He not only finished second in his main event but, more importantly to us media types, served as an interpreter for men's champion Lahliffi, who speaks little English," wrote reporter Dean Howe. "In fact, some reporters arriving late for the interview thought it was the 42-year-old Jaleta who earned the top Crim prize."

* * *

Until that point in his running career, Ted had been lucky to maintain his health. "The human body can adapt to anything," he says, thinking of the hundreds of kilometres of pounding the pavement that he's inflicted on his own body. "There's a risk of injury in any sport."

It happened to Ted in September 1997. He was nearing the end of the Minneapolis Marathon that snakes through the downtown area of the twin cities of Minneapolis and St. Paul, Minnesota. He was running alongside the river, glancing at the beautiful old brick buildings and the hundreds of people who lined the route to cheer on the runners.

There were only two miles left and he knew he was doing well. He was about to beat a Canadian Masters record for marathon distance.

"I was checking my watch. I was excited that I was on target to achieve the record," he recalls. "That excitement turned out to be a nightmare."

In a marathon, runners set a pace that is slightly slower than that of a 10K race because it must be maintained over a distance four times as long. Runners lock in at the same monotonous pace. Near the end of the race, it all comes down to endurance. Due to dehydration and the strain of long distance running, leg muscles are filled with lactic acid, a waste product that causes considerable pain at that point in the race. Ted ignored the pain and focused instead on a possible Canadian record. He wanted to stay with the group so he could sprint to the finish.

Just then, one of the front runners tried to surge ahead while going down a hill. Ted decided to follow him. It was a mistake.

All of a sudden, Ted felt a sharp pain shoot through his right thigh. He screamed in agony and dropped to the ground.

"The pain was excruciating. I couldn't even walk. I had to be taken away to the medical tent by ambulance."

He had torn a hamstring during that quick change of pace. The Canadian record was gone and so, too, perhaps, was any hope of further high-level competitive running. It was his first major injury and he thought his running career was over. He was devastated.

Ted didn't know how to deal with such a traumatic running injury and was depressed for some time. It was only the third time in his life that he had not finished a race. The first time was in Saskatoon in the late 1980s when the cold weather got to him. The second occasion was in Banff when he had an upset stomach.

While he was undergoing intensive therapy, he thought again about stopping competitive racing and maybe just running for fitness. He knew he would never run a marathon again. His sprinting ability was now restricted and he had to listen to his body.

The devastation of the injury lessened with time and almost disappeared completely when, a few months later, Ted was honoured with some of the most prestigious awards for his athletic achievements.

Runners World Magazine ranked him as number seven in the World in Masters Runners Men's 40-45 division in 1997. Had he participated in more international races, he might even have placed higher.

Ted also received the 1997 Saskatchewan Sport Athlete of the Year award for Male Masters in Athletics.

He was humbled and honoured by the international wins and by the world ranking. The award from SaskSport just put the icing on the cake. "I was recognized by the Saskatchewan sports community for my athletic achievements. Receiving that award gave me a great sense of pride. It confirmed my sense of belonging in this province."

Ted never did return to his old form or compete at that intensity again. However, he was still able to hold his own against the best in the world. In 1999, he competed in numerous races from the local to international level. He finished fifth in the 7.1 Mile Road Race in Falmouth, Massachusetts, where he had the opportunity, for the third or fourth time, to compete against one of his all-time running idols.

U.S. Olympic marathon champion Frank Shorter, who is seven years older than Ted, won the gold medal at the 1972 Olympic Games and the silver medal in the 1976 Olympics. "When I watched the Ethiopian runners in the 1972 Olympics on television, I saw Frank Shorter winning that race," recalls Ted. "Instantly, he became my hero. I dreamed to be like Frank and those other Olympians one day."

As an international Masters competitor, Ted loved running against Shorter and listening to him speak about his experiences. "His message was inspiring. It's kind of weird that when I started running in the Masters circuit in the U.S., I ended up running against Frank and others that I admired. Some of my heroes became my friends. Running with Frank was an incredible experience. He is one of the living legends and he is still my hero."

Ted notes that the world-calibre runners he has raced against are ordinary, everyday people except for their athletic abilities. "They work very hard, even though they are gifted. They have feelings and can get injured like anybody else. They're human. They are not invincible."

It is a testament to his sport, though, that a non-Olympian can run with the elite racers, Ted says proudly. "Running is the only sport that gives you an opportunity to compete against the best. You can line up with world record holders and run with them. Novice competitors can't play hockey with Wayne Gretzky or golf with Tiger Woods. That's the beauty of running."

Although Shorter has not known Ted for long, he appreciates Ted's stamina. "Ted is a great Masters runner. He must have some resiliency because he doesn't seem to repeatedly get hurt, and that's the major requirement to be able to do the kind of training you need to do at that level. And you need the right mental attitude," says Shorter.

"You have to know how to turn it on and turn it off. You can actually be very friendly with your opposition and then try to beat each other's brains out when you're competing. That's all part of the attraction of athletics, because you can be one way when you're competing and another way in other parts of your life."

Shorter says his best training partners were his rivals because they challenged him but also knew how to compete and still be friends. "One would be Steve Prefontaine, who got killed in an auto accident years ago. He was the best U.S. 5000-metre runner for a while."

Shorter believes that most Masters athletes at the international level are too intense off the field, viewing it as a job rather than the joy it should be. "Most of them competed when they were younger but didn't have the same relative success at the Masters level, whereas Ted had success so he understands that process of turning on and turning off, of focusing while competing and only while competing. Ted's got that ability more than pretty much any of the others out there. If you're going to compete against people, those are the people that I would fear because of their intensity while racing. The best compliment I could give is they're not the ones you want to see as you look around late in the race."

Another connection between Shorter and Ted is that both men greatly admire Abebe Bikila. "At the Olympics victory ceremony in 1972, Abebe Bikila was there in a wheelchair just before he died, and I met him right before the victory service," says Shorter. "Interesting parallel between Ted and I."

While Shorter was a good Masters athlete in his prime, he notes that Ted appears to have topped him. "When I became 40, I could run just about 30 minutes or a little over that time for 10,000 metres. When I was 48, that time would have probably gotten at least two minutes slower, maybe more. I'm not making excuses. That's the way it is. When I turned 40, I ran 9 minutes flat for 3000 metres."

At age 40, Ted ran 3000 metres in 8 minutes 52 seconds and in August 2004, at age 51, Ted finished a 10K race at 32:58 minutes. "He's about the same place I was except he's holding on a little better," states Shorter.

While Shorter estimates he has run 288,000 kilometres in his life, Ted has run at least 80,000 kilometres just around Wascana Centre park itself in Regina.

Ego is a large part of being a high-calibre runner and Shorter says he and Ted share a similar disposition in that respect. "My ego was not in it in that I needed to win. Your competition is always primarily against yourself. As long as you feel you're getting the most value out of it, that's what's important."

He and Ted both know how to keep a perspective that's uniquely their own as they have tried to keep their performance levels up. "You know your ability is going to go down. The fact that Ted can maintain it, that's what's incredible. I try to get slower as slowly as possible," adds Shorter, laughing.

At a Saskatchewan race in 2005, Ted came in first while a friend of his who is 18 years his junior came in second. The race results were in the newspaper and people congratulated Ted's friend, until they saw Ted's age. Then they teased him: "We didn't know you were competing with seniors."

Ted laughs at that comment and chuckles even longer when he reports on his friend's response to the teasing. "He just told them: 'Ted's a freak senior.' " Over the years, Ted has been called much worse than a 'freak senior' for his efforts as a runner, and he has no intentions of slowing down to accommodate others.

When reflecting on the successes of other high-level Masters athletes and his own success and desire to win at that level, Ted says it may be a matter of past achievements. "People like Frank Shorter have reached the highest level and maybe they're not as mentally hungry. What have they got to prove?"

Ted had missed out on his prime running years and felt he still had much to prove as an elite-level runner. "I believed in myself and that I had the ability to do it. All I needed was the opportunity. It is never too late to reach for one's goals," he says with intensity.

Ted's success as a runner in his later years, achieving better results at his age than Frank Shorter and others, is an indication that he likely would have done well as a young athlete. But no one will ever know for sure. When he won the junior nationals in Ethiopia, Ted was the fastest runner on the field that day, beating a future Olympian, and he wasn't even trained to his peak performance level.

Ted's running career ended early, but so did those of many other young Ethiopian athletes because of civil unrest and lack of opportunity. "That situation affected everyone, not just me. Many young people faced the same tragedy and missed out on a promising future."

Shorter isn't sure if Ted would have ever been an Olympian, but says it is sad that he did not get the chance. "You don't know. You can't speculate on when you're going to level off, and part of the fun is just finding how high you can go. He would have been willing to try. That's another attribute he has that a lot of athletes don't have. It's that willingness and that life commitment to the training and the focus to be able to do it just to find out, so that you never have to say at some point in your life: 'Well, if only I had kept going and seen what would have happened.' To me, it's a tragedy that he never got to find out."

Ted agrees that the willingness to try is essential. "If you don't have a desire to explore your potential, you'll never know how good you can be. I have seen many talented individuals who lack the desire to follow their dreams. They dream about being a doctor, a sports star or a famous person, but they don't apply themselves to achieve that goal. It means hard work, discipline and commitment. If you are good at something and work hard to reach your goal, anything is possible," Ted believes. "If you don't, you are restricting the options for your future."

* * *

Some of Ted's warmest memories while training come from times when he looked over to see his son Adam either running or riding a bicycle beside him during warm-up and cool-down runs. When Adam was 10 years old, he ran up and down the hills around the town of Lumsden to train with his father. "The next day, he was walking funny. I asked what was wrong and he said his butt was sore," laughs Ted.

Adam took up running as a sport for a while when he was in Grades 7 and 8. Ted fondly recalls one day when the two of them participated in the same track meet. They both won for their age groups and their names appeared in the same newspaper column. "That was a wonderful moment," says the proud father.

As Adam grew older, his enthusiasm for the sport waned and his dad supported him in his decision to find another interest. "I could sense he was struggling to tell me that he did not want to run. He did not want to hurt my feelings," recalls Ted. "I advised him to follow his heart's desire and try to do well." From Grade 9 on, Adam played basketball and other team sports.

Another enjoyable aspect of Ted's high-calibre racing has been the number of fans who recognize him on the street and circle around him with papers in hand, asking for his autograph. The requests started coming in the late 1980s in Canada after he had made a name for himself in Saskatchewan and Alberta, and intensified once he began racing in the U.S.

Volunteers who came to pick him up at U.S. airports often asked for his autograph. Invited runners were required to sign race posters in the hospitality rooms prior to races and to attend autograph and media sessions the day before the race. Ted would also be stopped during warm-up and cool-down periods and at award ceremonies by fans and other distance runners who asked him to sign their bib numbers. In Canada, people called out to him on the street or in malls.

Ted is not one to request or require adoration, but says these moments of fame were appreciated. "It was great to be one of the champions among that select group of invited athletes signing autographs. It was an incredible uplifting feeling. You never know where life's destiny will take you. Looking back, I'm proud of what I have done. I enjoyed every moment of it."

Ted also recalls a few times when he was invited to the podium to make an impromptu speech after winning a race. At awards ceremonies, he would be asked to say a few words, usually thanking the organizers of the event and talking briefly about his experience during the race.

For Ted, running against world-calibre athletes was a pleasant ride. Those dreams of reaching the podium that he had long ago, while he was lying on the ground in that filthy refugee camp, had finally come true.

He had run for fun and friendship and he had found glory.

CHAPTER ELEVEN

REVISITING THE PAST

By the late 1990s, Ethiopia's political situation had stabilized enough that it was safe for Ted to return to his homeland. It would be his first visit since he fled in 1978.

He was anxious and excited but also a little worried about the reaction he would get from his family. Even though they had been corresponding, Ted wasn't sure how they really felt about him after his long absence.

"I was scared to face them. They endured such hardship because of me. I wasn't sure they would accept me or love me."

He arrived at the Addis Ababa airport around 11 o'clock at night and was not greeted in the airport as is common in North America. Only passengers and airport employees were allowed inside the terminal. The airport was run down and the computer system was not working, so Ted had to wait while airport staff manually tried to locate his luggage. By the time he found out that his luggage had not been transferred from the previous flight connecting at Frankfurt and that he would have to come back to pick it up days later when the next flight came in, Ted had been on the ground for an hour. Finally, he grabbed his backpack and walked outside into the dark night.

As he approached the gates leading to the street, he saw about 20 people huddled together, some of whom he recognized from photos. His brothers, sisters, nieces and nephews were all standing there, waiting to greet him. One nephew held a large sign with Ted's name on it and a niece immediately handed Ted a large bouquet of flowers.

"Everyone ran to me. We were all crying tears of joy and hugging each other," Ted recalls.

The family had to rent three vans to get to the hotel where Ted would stay for the next seven weeks. Everyone packed into his small hotel room and visited for about an hour. They asked him questions about his life and hugged him. He tried to find out all the names of his nieces and nephews and started catching up on 21 years.

At about one o'clock in the morning, most of Ted's relatives left, except for two brothers and two nephews who stayed overnight and slept on a couch and second bed. The next morning, they all travelled to the home of one of his sisters, where Ted's elderly father was recovering from a broken hip. It was not a big house and it was packed with people, all of whom wiped away tears of joy for at least an hour. Ted recalls the thrill of looking around to see his siblings, nieces, nephews and father.

"It was amazing. Some of my younger siblings teased me about growing up in the Stone Age. They couldn't believe how far we used to walk."

Ted's siblings were quick to tell him that they were still not sure how he had survived the ordeals he encountered. "My siblings shook their heads and asked how I did it. They think I am superhuman, but I am not. I just have a strong will to live. I shared my determination not to give up or to be crushed."

Ted had figured out ways to cope on his own and survive in a lonely environment. Being back in Ethiopia felt so much better than that. "It was great to be surrounded with my siblings and my dad for those weeks. The warm family love was an unbelievable feeling. Wow! That had been missing for so many years."

Ted was also amazed and overwhelmed by the physical changes in Ethiopia since he had been gone. Highways had replaced the dirt paths he had run on and many of the trees and forests that existed when he was a child had been cleared to make room for development. There were bridges over patches of water that had been impassable in Ted's youth, and schools were now in every region compared to the scattered number of facilities that existed in the 1960s and 1970s. Females were now included among the most educated leaders in the communities, a fact that was much appreciated by this champion of women's rights.

One of the more difficult periods of Ted's 1999 trip to Ethiopia was the stark realization that his mother was dead.

"It really hit me when I got there. She has always been kind of an umbrella, sheltering everyone. Not having her there was very difficult."

Ted also had to deal with the devastating loss of his sister Sadate. Even though it had been six years since she had died from breast cancer, the pain was as real for Ted as though he had heard the news that very day. "She was the first in my immediate family to pass away since I left Ethiopia. That was very hard."

Even now, Ted wipes away tears when he thinks about Sadate.

She, above all others, was the person in his family that he trusted most when he was in hiding. She never told his secrets to anyone else, even when she was later questioned by authorities. She had been a brave young girl who took many risks to help and protect her oldest brother. Ted still admires her courage and will always miss her.

Ted did not visit his home village because there was still concern about his safety there. Instead, family members travelled to visit him in Addis Ababa. The capital city itself brought back some painful memories, though.

When walking through the streets, Ted saw military personnel carrying AK-47 automatic rifles. The sight made him uneasy and heightened the sense of loss he felt in not being able to find any of the people with whom he had grown up. Most of them had either left the country or died.

As he looked around, Ted felt empty and disconnected from the land of his birth. "There was a new generation now. I was just a tourist. Belonging is not a land or a building. You have to feel it. That brought a kind of closure in my mind to know I did not really belong there any more."

Sometimes when Ted talks about Ethiopia today, a glazed look comes over his face and those in his presence can see that his mind is drifting back in time. There is a profound sadness in his eyes, reminiscent of the scared teenager who ran away from death. One can almost see an imaginary wall form around his physical body, protecting him from further harm. This subtle change in personality lasts for only a split second, though, because Ted does not allow himself to dwell on the past.

One of Ted's proudest memories from his 1999 trip to Ethiopia was seeing the positive results of the financial assistance he had provided over the years to at least 15 of his family members. These included the children of the uncle who had assisted him in high school.

For years, Ted had encouraged his younger relatives to get an education. Every country, no matter the political system, needs educated people, he told them. Ted was pleased that he was fortunate enough to be able to send money to assist them in those pursuits. "It is part of our culture. We have an obligation to help family members who are struggling," he explains. He wouldn't have it any other way.

Ted relished the moments spent with his nieces and nephews, hearing the stories of their achievements. One of his nieces is a judge in a lower district court. He teased her that she might have to use her authority to keep her uncle in line while he was in the country. Ted asked if she would put him in jail if he did something to get arrested. She told him she didn't think he was the kind of person who would commit petty crimes but if he did, he would have to pay for the crime. "That's her job. I admire that. That's a bold statement," says the proud uncle.

Another niece, who has become an authority figure in her community, lamented to her uncle that she was not yet married. She wondered why he thought that was so. Ted told her: "Maybe it's because men are intimidated by you. Don't settle for less."

Ted proudly notes that some of his other nieces are nurses and teachers. One nephew is a judge, two are schoolteachers and another is a lawyer. All have at least a Grade 12 education and are doing well. "It was rewarding to be with them and share in their achievements. When I left Ethiopia, some of them were little children. I enjoyed having an opportunity to get to know them as adults."

Many of Ted's siblings have since died. Sadly, the average life expectancy in Ethiopia is 50 years old. Some, however, are working on their Masters or Administration degrees and Ted couldn't be more proud of them. He's happy they've tasted what education can do for them in terms of freedom and monetary rewards.

Ted also spent some time training with the national running team during his 1999 trip. "I was a big shot runner in Canada at that time," he says with a smile. "I connected with some of the athletes and went running with them."

On his first time out, he lasted only half an hour before he had to stop running. Ted was no longer used to that high altitude and couldn't get enough oxygen into his lungs to keep running. He knew that it had nothing to do with his level of fitness. He had to acclimatize.

He ran with the male members of the Ethiopian national team for three mornings until they suggested that maybe he should step down a notch and run with the elite females until he was able to build up his conditioning enough to keep up with the men. When he went running with the women, he struggled to keep up with them, too.

While he may not have excelled immediately on the training course, Ted certainly appreciated his surroundings while he ran. "There's a beautiful forest around the city and mountains in the background. It was so nice. Addis Ababa is almost 8,000 feet above sea level and when you're running on the hills, you can climb up another 2,000 feet and feel the change in the layers of air. You can see the whole city from there."

Ted ran three mornings a week with the national teams and on his own on the other days. Finally, when he went for a workout, he managed to progress to the middle of the pack of male runners, which was quite a thrill. He was old enough to be their father.

The world-class runners Ted met on that trip asked him plenty of questions about his life in Canada. What does he eat? What does he do when he's not running? Ted was pleased to share his knowledge and learn more about the science of running from them. When he asked them for training secrets, they told him not to set barriers on his running and to work hard. These were lessons Ted had already been using for years in his running and in his life.

* * *

In 2002, Ted travelled to Ethiopia again, this time for a two-week visit. This trip was taken mainly to pay tribute to a brother who had died that spring. One of the highlights of the journey was the precious time spent with his aging father.

"It was wonderful to see my father once more before he died the following year at the age of 92. During our final visit, he reflected on his parenting and the effect he had on his children. He regretted that he had not fulfilled his parental obligations and encouraged me to pursue my dreams for education and sports. That bothered him for a long time. I was able to reassure him that I forgave him for any misgivings he had, and that I knew he had done what he thought was right at the time. This discussion brought peace to both of us."

Ted believes it is important to forgive in order to heal. "It wasn't my parents' fault," he says of the unrest in the 1970s. "It was something we could not avoid. As a parent myself, I know what my dad was feeling. Every parent questions his or her own parenting skills. Some children believe that they have an absolute right to certain things from their parents, like a car or other expensive material things. I believe the parents' obligation is to provide the basic needs and steer the child in the right direction. Beyond that, the children should be striving to achieve any privileged materials on their own. I never demanded extras from my parents. I always believed that I was the solution for my own life."

On this trip to Ethiopia, Ted was more comfortable than he had been in 1999. "It was easier this time to face all the hurt and destruction from the past. During this trip, we reminisced a lot about the good and bad times. We laughed and cried. My family told me I was more relaxed this time. During my 1999 trip, I was tense. I woke up with nightmares of being chased. This time was much better."

In 2002, Ted also knew that political changes were occurring in the country of his birth and it gave him a more peaceful feeling. He learned that former security personnel who had terrorized him and others in the 1970s were now in prison and being dealt with. Ethiopia still has its social economic problems, like many other countries including those in North America, but Ted could see the progress from his first trip. "We did not talk about Ethiopian politics. We talked about Canada. It's not fair for me to comment on the current situation there. I have left it behind."

Prior to this trip, one of Ted's brothers met a businessman who had been a classmate of Ted's from Grade 4 on. Ted's brother arranged for the man to meet Ted at his hotel. It was an emotional reunion.

"When we first saw each other, we each started crying tears of joy," recalls Ted. "He was feeling my face with his hands, saying: 'Is that you? Is that you?' He couldn't believe I was real."

Ted himself was having some trouble comprehending the sight of his friend from the past. "I thought he was dead. I was shocked to see him."

The two men spent the rest of the day together, exchanging stories of what each of them had done and what had happened to some of their other acquaintances during that period. The businessman also connected Ted with another friend that Ted had not seen since he left Ethiopia. Ted learned that both of his friends had been in prison for several years without being charged. They had both been tortured as well. Both men were now making a good living in Ethiopia.

Ted had wondered about the fate of these two friends for many years. He was relieved to share an embrace and breathe easily again with two long-lost, now happy friends.

Chapter Twelve

A Coach And Leader

In the year 2000, Ted decided to hang up his international competitive racing shoes. His priorities had changed and he had achieved his goals in athletics. He was tired of the travelling and wanted to focus on other things. Running had been and would continue to be his life, however. "The beauty of running is it's not as time-consuming as team sports," he said at the time. "You can get a good workout in 30 minutes. You can run any time anywhere. I will be doing it for fitness for the rest of my life."[27]

Ted looked forward instead to spending more time with his son, who had started Grade 9 that year. "Adam has been the one thing that has kept Ted in Regina when he maybe had opportunities to go elsewhere," says Darren Burrows. "There's nothing that's made him prouder than to watch Adam be involved in his sports and to have him around."

Since Adam's birth, Ted had tried to spend as much time as he could with his son. It wasn't always possible because of Ted's busy schedule and other commitments Adam had with his mother and her family.

Ted admits he is not perfect when it comes to raising Adam, and there have been typical father-son disagreements over chores and sleeping hours, for example. There were also times when the two did not see each other for months because of family disputes.

Adam says the relationship between he and his father is more like that of two friends than it is of parent and son. Adam grew up in his mother's home but Ted has been an active part of Adam's life, as his parent and chauffeur for many events. Their relationship grew even stronger after Adam turned 16. He began spending more time with his dad and then moved in with him.

Adam remembers going on trips as a child with his father to visit the huge West Edmonton Mall and to Calgary and Banff. He also remembers visiting the northern Saskatchewan town of Nipawin as well, where they fished and ripped through the evergreen forest on the backs of two motocross bikes. Hanging out in the living room of his dad's place with Ted and some of Ted's younger running buddies was more common. Adam is still thankful that his father had some younger friends. "I'd play video games with Darren and those guys. My dad couldn't do it. He couldn't figure it out. He was totally dumbfounded by that stuff."

Ted agrees that he and technology don't always get along. "My typing skills are so bad. I still type like this," he says, doing a perfect impression of a two-finger typist.

Ted beams when he talks about watching Adam become a fine young football player and star basketball player who helped Regina's Balfour Collegiate win the 2004 city and provincial high school basketball championships. "Some of the greatest moments for me have been watching him play. I get satisfaction when he reaches his goal and is happy. Regardless of his sporting activities, he will always be the most important person in my life. I don't know what my life would be like without him."

When the Balfour Redmen won the Saskatchewan High School Athletic Association 5A Boys Basketball Championship in March 2004, Adam was the highest scorer with a total of 29 points. The team won the game 98 – 91. Ted couldn't sleep when Adam's team won the provincial title because he was so excited for his son.

As a parent sitting in the stands, Ted is not one to make a big fuss during a game. Some parents yell. Ted doesn't like to interfere, which follows his own philosophy of how to be a successful coach. "As a coach, you have to be positive and encourage them, to get the best out of themselves as athletes."

Adam appreciates his father's support but says that all the commotion surrounding his dad's own achievements is sometimes hard to swallow. "The way people see my dad and the way I see my dad are two different things. To me, he's just my dad," says the 19-year-old, who has more characteristics in common with his father than he might care to admit.

"I hear it so many times, it doesn't have an effect on me," Adam says about his father's running awards. "I still care for it. He does try to motivate me to do the same things he does for other people. Of course, you're not always going to see eye to eye with your parents."

Over the years, Ted has encouraged his son to be polite, have good manners, keep his room clean and use his time wisely. He is frustrated by Canadian teenagers he has met who do nothing but party and sleep all weekend, then are tired when they go to work or school on Monday. "I'm not saying: 'Don't have fun.' Do so in moderation and fulfill your responsibilities."

Ted admits that when he suggests to youth that they are "missing out" by partying or sleeping too much, he rarely gets a good response. "They think I'm a lunatic."

Adam understands why his dad thinks the way he does about why Canadian children should appreciate what they have. It's just hard to apply that to real life some days. "The way we are raised and the way he was raised are two different things," says the son.

Ted's mentorship has had a lasting impact on Adam. It is obvious as Adam spins off a list of all the things he has learned from his father: "Perseverance, not giving up, handling defeat, taking your losses and learning from them. To get to where my dad is, you have to persevere a lot. He had to go through a lot of rejection. Sometimes I feel that with my basketball," adds Adam, who made it as far as the last cut of the University of Regina team. "People still say I'm good enough to play."

Adam has the Jaleta genes in him and is not about to give up on his goal of playing at a higher level. "My dad was 29 years old when he started running again. That's supposed to be when people start to decline as athletes. People say to my dad: 'You have to quit acting half your age. You're 51 years old.' My dad's still young at heart. I think it's hilarious when other runners who are way younger than my dad tell me my dad can beat them in a race. You yourself don't know the whole potential you're ever going to reach," says Adam.

"My dad could have not hopped that fence or given up in that refugee camp. You have to keep on going. You gotta put that effort in to be able to withstand," adds Adam, echoing his father's philosophy for life.

Adam is truly his father's son in one other respect. "I'm opinionated. You have to have your opinion about things. You can't fall in line. You have to be your own person."

* * *

Since 1991, Ted has coached teenage and adult long distance runners with the Wheat City track club. He wanted to give something back to the sport that he loves and felt he could be a good role model for other athletes.

In 2004, he started coaching the men's cross-country and track and field teams at the University of Regina, adding that to his Wheat City club duties. In the years in between and since, Ted has offered individual instruction or suggestions to runners from ages 13 and up who run at all levels from recreational to competitive events such as the national championships and Canada Summer Games. On any given day, he might have 10 to 20 athletes seeking his advice.

At least three times a week, he coaches the combined group of University and Wheat City runners for at least two hours. They run their own programs for the rest of the week. On Sunday mornings, Ted either runs with the athletes or watches them run. "When I'm coaching in the base season while runners are building up their endurance, I run with them. When they are working towards a competition, that is serious and I have to watch them. I go earlier and do my own run and wait for them, or I do my run afterwards."

As a long distance running coach, there are few more revered by athletes of all ages and abilities in Regina than Ted. After the 2006 Regina Police Service Half Marathon, Ted was invited to address the 800 athletes and supporters gathered at the brunch for the awards presentations. The room at the Centre of the Arts was abuzz with people noisily exchanging their stories of triumph and pain from the morning run.

Until Ted approached the microphone. Then the room was suddenly quiet.

Ted thanked his listeners for their attention that day and encouraged them in their efforts to stay fit and enjoy the great sport of running. He barely mentioned the struggles of his background and he offered a few training tips for his audience. Many of the people in the room had heard Ted speak before and had already benefited from his running expertise as well.

During the awards presentations, male and female athletes stopped at Ted's table to shake his hand or give him a hug on their way up to the podium to collect their medals. They thanked him for contributing to their success, as did a middle-aged man who approached Ted after the brunch. "I just came back from the Boston Marathon. I had a good race. I couldn't have done it without you," the man told Ted.

This response from athletes is one that Ted thoroughly enjoys. "One of the rewards of coaching is seeing athletes achieve their goals. When they smile, you cannot equate that with money."

At the University of Regina indoor track on a Saturday morning, several young athletes approach Ted for advice. They ask about their time during a particular lap and which shoes and spikes they should wear for certain conditions. What should they do with a particular leg injury and how many minutes should they spend on the exercise bike after their run? Ted remembers the details of each of their latest races, knows each of their individual running programs and their goals for the short term and longer.

While the athletes run on the track that circles around the top of a basketball court in the Kinesiology building at the University of Regina, Sandy Bain talks about why he is interested in following Ted's example to become a coach. "The neat thing about Ted is, he's a coach but he's also a training partner, too," says Bain, who graduated from the University of Regina Cougar long distance runner program in 2006.

"When we do workouts, Ted does the workout, too. It's more motivating because you might be hurting, but he's right there with you doing it, telling you to go faster. He's a great mentor. He's taught me a lot of different things about running that I didn't know before. I've seen great results in the cross-country season and I've been getting personal bests."

Alicia Roske and Curtis Koskie are two other students who have benefitted from Ted's ability to quickly assess talent and potential in runners. "I think he sees things in people, because when I started training with him, he knew something good was going to come out of it," says Roske. If she had not been injured twice in two years, Roske would have been competing at a higher level more quickly, but she has no intention of quitting now.

She says Ted was particularly devastated about her second injury, a broken bone in her foot. "He couldn't sleep that night because he was so worried." Ted helped her recover and encouraged her to overcome her setback. "It's all him. He's keeping me going, because quitting was definitely an option at that point."

Ted first saw Curtis Koskie at a basketball camp when he was in Grade 9. Ted said to Curtis' mother at the time: "He's a runner, not a basketball player."

When looking at individuals to determine if they could be competitive runners, Ted checks their physical stature and their attributes as a runner. "I can sense, looking at them, and also I can see in their eyes if they have the desire to excel and the commitment to discipline," he explains.

In Koskie's case, Ted was also being practical. "I don't like to see people wasting time at things they are not good at," says the man who learned that lesson while sitting on a soccer bench as a child. Ted suggested that Curtis realistically consider his future prospects in basketball, knowing that he isn't even six feet tall. "Curtis is a good runner. We planned when he would be great." With Ted's coaching, Curtis won the cross-country high school provincials and 3000-metre event. He also gained a university scholarship.

Ted's actions in the lives of these young athletes follow his philosophy of strong leadership. "My role is to make them understand that there will always be setbacks in life. It won't be as smooth as we might wish. We learn from these setbacks and keep striving towards our goal, and we'll do it together. This can be applied in relationships at home, at work or anywhere."

Knowing a bit about Ted's past has helped his athletes get a different perspective on their own gifts. "No matter how much I'm hurting, he's been in a lot worse situations. So that just drives me to keep going," says Roske.

Curtis Koskie considers Ted his coach and his friend. "He's like my family, too. He cares about his athletes. Huge."

The bond between him and Ted may be more pronounced because of Koskie's history as a cancer survivor. Koskie was diagnosed with a brain tumour in 1990 and has been cancer-free since 1991, but the lasting effects include some loss of physical flexibility and an occasional bout of social and emotional turmoil.

"Ted Jaleta has been a godsend to us for our son," says Maxine Koskie, Curtis' mother. "The time Curtis needed it most is when Ted appeared. He has helped Curtis with meeting people, socializing and reading people correctly." Maxine adds that Ted treats all his runners the same.

"He works a lot with them on mental and visual positive self-image. He tries to get them to relax. He supports them in their diets. He coaches his athletes to help them be lifelong athletes. He looks at their futures."

Ted reluctantly accepts praise for his coaching techniques. He is simply passing on what he learned as a young runner in Ethiopia. "I was taught not to put barriers on myself when I run. We don't even talk about winning or being a famous Olympian. Of course, you can always have a dream to be that, but if you do the work, good results will come later. You have to have a passion first and believe in yourself and want to win. There are no shortcuts."

Ted follows a specific philosophy with his athletes. Coaching alone will not create miraculous results. Athletes must possess an inner drive to win and Ted's role as a coach is to try to support and encourage them, creating a positive environment for them to experience growth while reaching for their goals. "I teach them to learn from me but not to depend on me. I don't run for them. They run themselves. I know they can do it."

Ted is not one who tolerates tardiness. "In Ethiopia, if you get invited for supper, you can show up an hour late and still get a meal. I prefer to be at least five minutes early. If people come late without reason, I am irritated." Students who arrive late for a training session with Ted might find themselves staying afterwards by themselves to finish their program. "When I commit, I take my responsibilities very seriously and I expect my athletes to do so as well."

Marion Craig is another testament to Ted's coaching skills. She was an accomplished high school track star who went on to participate in races, triathlons, cross-country skiing and the Discovery Channel Eco-Challenge, among other events. As she approached her 40th birthday, Craig asked for Ted's assistance to help her get back to being the super-competitive athlete she had always been.

Ted noticed that her energy was divided among too many activities and convinced her that if she focused instead on only running, she would achieve better results. "Coaching is not only technical planning. You must make them believe they can do it and provide the leadership so they can reach their potential," he explains. "She stuck with it when she saw the results."

"There's an instant respect that's gained when an athlete knows the coach has been there, done that," says Craig, a Royal Canadian Mounted Police sergeant. "What makes Ted different is he's probably been the highest-quality athlete I've had as a coach. I don't think he should be winning all the local races at age 50, but he does win. I certainly find that motivating."

Craig remembers her first performance at a workout with coach Jaleta. "I was a complete disaster. I started out way too fast. The way he dealt with me was that it was an inexperienced faux pas. I bounced right back." Within two years of turning 40 and thus becoming a Masters runner, Craig held the indoor Saskatchewan Masters records for 600, 800, 1000 and 3000 metres. "Ted brought me to that level, after 20 years away from the track. I have to credit that to Ted Jaleta."

Craig also says Ted showed her genuine care and interest, which are two marks of a good coach and leader. "He's very intense and encouraging at races. If he's not there, we communicate right after the race. He always listens to his athletes and he has a good way of remembering details as well. He'll even remember races from last year."

An athlete who mentions being tired may actually be complaining of a sore leg that could foreshadow a serious injury. Ted's experience as a runner and coach enables him to recognize that cry for help, listening to the spoken and unspoken signals from each athlete. "He believes in a formality about things," says Craig, who became a coach with both the Wheat City club and the University of Regina under Ted's tutelage. "When somebody's come back from a race, Ted remembers and, at the next practice, he recognizes their performance."

Jason Warick agrees. "Ted always remembers the small things. If I go off to a race, he'll always call me or e-mail me, look up my result on the Internet and congratulate me or console me. Well after he retired, I finally broke one of his records in the 10K in the province. He was one of the first people to call me. It was real genuine happiness," says Warick.

"When I look around Regina at the track, all the kids look up to him. Everybody respects him. He's got a real magnetic personality. People just like to hang out with him. He's a really nice guy. Part of why he gets a lot done is he's so likeable. It's sincere. It's not a put-on."

Craig believes that Ted's history plays a large role in his present-day coaching techniques. "To win the Ethiopian national high school championships, it's probably not too long before he would have gone to the Olympic trials. I believe Ted would have been on that path had he not had some other huge issues in his life. What carried him through all of that wartime, persecution and leaving his country was, he maintained that passion."

* * *

One of the things Craig really likes about Ted's coaching philosophy is: "He will get the athlete working as hard as they think they can and then he will say: 'You think it's over. I want you to do one more.'"

She recalls the first time Ted pulled that trick on her. "I finished a 5K time trial and Ted said: 'Good. I'll give you a minute break and I'd like another mile as fast as you can go. I just want to show you how much you have left.' I could have sworn I ran that as fast as I could," Craig recalls thinking. She then ran again and surprised herself with her effort.

"He could have said to me: 'You're not running as hard as you can.' But he didn't. Having had that experience, I can train faster when I go to do my intervals. He has an ability to present situations like that. He will set up the workout and the experience where you figure it out."

Ted has often invited committed recreational runners into the track club to encourage them to pursue a life of fitness. Their skill level is immaterial to him. He welcomes them into the group and accepts them for who they are and their interest in running, says Craig. "He doesn't see that as an impediment in his coaching."

Craig tells the athletes she coaches: "This is a 52-week-a-year project you're embarking on, to have a lifestyle of fitness." She adds that: "Ted reflects that incredibly well in what he does, how he cares for his body."

* * *

Dr. Christina Vuksic had run in two marathons before contacting Ted in 2000 for some private coaching lessons to help her qualify to run in the Boston Marathon.

"What I discovered is, Ted coaches on his vast experience and his guts," says Vuksic. "With him, it's an art form. A lot of coaches use tables. They talk about the oxygen mass, physiological parameters, aerobic threshold training, that sort of thing. Although Ted used the terminology, he coached purely on his gut, his absolute experience and knowledge, and his sense of how fast someone could run."

Ted gave Vuksic instructions on how to train and also ran with her most of the time. "He ran just in front of me and the whole time he'd say things like: 'You can do this. We're going to do this in 6.58 minutes.' And when he got tired of talking, he'd whistle like he was whistling for a dog, which made me want to kill him but actually I would run faster. He called me an athlete and made me feel for the first time that I was an athlete. I was a 40-year-old woman at the time. This was like my midlife crisis. I was having the most wonderful time of my life and it was hard. Very, very hard."

Vuksic qualified for the marathon and arrived in Boston with Ted's vision of her abilities in her head. Ted told Vuksic she should aim for a time of three hours and 20 minutes. Prior to the race, she had arranged to go for dinner in Boston with some other runners from Saskatchewan. Vuksic had not met them before that night and recalls that they were all amazed when she told them the time she was intending to run.

"Silence fell around the table and one fellow said: 'Really? You think you're going to run that?' That was the first hint I had that maybe that was not really possible," she laughs, adding that she ran the race exactly as Ted had instructed her to run it. The start was slower than expected so she had to speed up for a while to catch her required time. She crossed the finish line in 3:21.02, only one minute past her anticipated goal, "and there wasn't a moment that Ted and his coaching were not in my mind and in my watch." She then phoned Ted at work to report in after the race.

"He tells me that when I phoned, he got up and was dancing this little victory dance. His boss walked in and asked what he was doing and Ted said: 'Well, Chris, my athlete, just ran the Boston Marathon in 3:21.02!' That's how he is, so connected with his athletes."

With Ted's prodding, Vuksic has since become one of Saskatchewan's top female Masters long distance runners and a long distance coach with the Wheat City track club. She has also become his friend, as have the other members of the Vuksic family – her husband Stan, who is also a physician and long distance runner, and their three children Megan, Jovan and Tim. "We'd share stories and tears," says Chris about her family's times with Ted. "We'd have him over for dinner. Stan equally found him to be a person of great quality and depth."

Ted coached Stan for a while and also added Jovan to his list of student athletes. With Ted's guidance, Jovan won the bantam boys Saskatchewan provincial cross-country championship and every meet at the high school local and provincial levels when he was in Grades 9 and 10. "In those two years, he broke four indoor midget men's provincial records," says Chris. "He went to junior nationals and finished sixth in 19-and-under in Canada in 5000 metres. He was 15 years old. Jovan will tell you that 50% of that was Ted."

Chris believes that Ted's coaching strategy brings out the best in his athletes. "He used to tell my son he was teaching him to run like an Ethiopian, and he did. He taught Jovan not to be afraid to make running a daily event and to understand that, at that age, he could run gradually and safely for miles without causing himself harm. He kept him in races that were appropriate to his age group."

In 2002, Jovan Vuksic set the midget men's provincial records in 800, 1000, 1500, and 3000 metres. "In the next year, my son started to love cars more than running. That was hard for us but you have to be happy in what you do," explains Chris, noting that Ted fully supported Jovan's decision and encouraged him to pursue an education and continue to run for fitness.

"Ted never lost sight of what was important to my son. That was something that touched me greatly. He never made him feel bad for making a different choice. Ted still believes that Jovan will some day run again."

One of the key aspects of Ted's coaching of students is that he insists running be only a part of their lives. "I advise my university runners to be student athletes, not athlete students. Education has to be their first priority. They can run later in life. Education is one of the most powerful tools to live a fulfilling life. If you combine education and sports, you cannot lose."

Ted's other main message to students is to strive for what they are most interested in and what they do best. "Be who you are, to get the best out of yourself, whatever the circumstances are socially, politically, spiritually."

* * *

When Megan Vuksic was in Grade 12, she and her mother were both coached by Ted. One day, they ended up running against each other in the same 1500-metre indoor race because there were no events in their own age groups. Chris and Megan went head-to-head in the "race to end all races" that has become a favourite Vuksic family story.

Ted gave both competitors his last-minute words of advice and as usual, he held nothing back, Chris says. "He's a 'take-no-prisoners' kind of guy. He believes women don't understand the idea of friendly competition as well as men do. When you get into competition, you should fight to the death. You can be friends with someone but there's no nice guy in a race. You go for the win."

Ted had taught Chris specific race strategies such as how to surge on someone when it's going to discourage them the most. "He was teaching my daughter the same stuff," Chris adds with a grin.

The two women lined up at the start, wished each other a good race and were off. Chris couldn't believe her eyes. She was running hard but lap after lap, her daughter was right behind her. "Megan was dogging my heels. She was this far away from me the whole race," explains Chris, holding her fingers centimetres apart. "Up until that time I was beating her in workouts."

Megan had fixed her mother's short hair into 'puppy tails' before the race and afterwards told her mom what was going through her mind while she was running. "She was thinking: 'I'll pace my mom and that will give me my personal best,' because she knew what I would run. At that time, I was running 5:25 minutes in that event. She was running after me thinking: 'There's those puppy tails.' It's seven and a half laps around the indoor track. We're racing our hearts out, we're dying out there, and as we get to about the fourth lap, Megan was thinking: 'I hate those puppy tails, I hate those puppy tails! I'm going to get that woman!' " Chris laughs.

"The crowd was into it and Ted was just going crazy, telling both of us to totally kick butt. He's taking turns. He's saying to Megan: 'You can pass her, Megan, you can do it!' And he's saying to me: 'Stay ahead of her, Chris!' "

They didn't win the race but that didn't matter. Mother and daughter had a photo finish, with Megan beating her mom by a hundredth of a second. "No matter what else happened, we ended up passing several university girls and doing quite well in that race because we were so totally into this dog-eat-dog competition," says Chris.

"That was an incredible moment. I love my daughter very much. We're quite close. We were both just crying at the end. We had our arms around each other," says Chris, who pauses again to savour the memory. "Another moment provided by Ted Jaleta, as far as I'm concerned."

Chris says Ted kept track of Megan's running exploits when she was away at university and trained her when she was home on school breaks. "She absolutely adores him. She phones him after her races."

The youngest Vuksic boy has also been affected by Ted, not only through his love for running with the Wheat City track club but in his view of the world around him. "We went out for dinner as a family and we were talking about freedom of speech," explains Chris. "My 13-year-old son went into an impassioned dissertation about freedom of speech and why it's so important to live in a democracy, because it allows you to speak what you think, no matter what anyone else thinks of that. That came directly from being around Ted," says Chris. "Ted changes lives and that's really important. That's what it's about."

On the more humourous side of their relationship with Ted, Chris recalls one of Ted's less accomplished sporting moments. "We've taken him skating. That was one of our funniest experiences. Think of how good he is at running. That's how bad he is at skating."

* * *

Ted can be very demanding at times, says Jason Warick, who sees it as one of Ted's strengths. "He definitely expects a lot from people. If he's coaching you or training with you, then he'll expect you to put in the effort he's putting in. If you're not, he'll find out why. If that effort doesn't come, he'll move on to someone that needs his help. He focuses his attention on the places he thinks he can do the most good. If he does commit and some of the athletes don't work to their potential, it's really hard on him."

Ted has coached a couple of talented athletes who, for one reason or another, didn't want to make a strong commitment to running. Eventually, they just fell away from the sport. "When Ted sees people that have a gift and don't use it, that's one of the things that hurts him most," explains Warick. "If you're willing to do the work, he can be a real advocate for you."

Those around Ted will not often hear a negative word from him. He prefers instead to focus on the positive and point out weaknesses in a way that does not lower another person's self esteem. "If you talk only pessimistically, they are just crushed," he says of people he is trying to help. "Even in the workplace, people should not just dwell on weaknesses. Talk about strengths, too, and help others to do better."

Ted is unbelievably kind. When faced with a situation that would cause most people to become annoyed or raise their voice in anger, Ted somehow manages to rise above that. The most that he will ever say is that he is frustrated or disappointed. He reminds himself that the person who is causing the frustrations has some good qualities. He thinks through the situation and looks for a solution that will not diminish anyone in the process.

In the case of his student athletes, Ted will phrase his comments with a positive twist. "I can see you have a natural gift and an ability to achieve. We have a goal to reach this level based on your potential and these are the things we need to do," he'll say. He will then record his statements and help the athletes, one step at a time, to achieve those goals. Several months later, he will go back to each person with the recorded statements and help them see their progress.

Ted occasionally teases his athletes with a proverb used by African runners. The proverb roughly translates to: 'Don't get behind while running, because if you get behind, you'll be eaten by a lion.'

The story goes that when you wake up on the African plains, you'd better be running fast because you have to outrun your enemy. In order to survive there, gazelles have to run faster than lions. If a lion can't outrun the slowest gazelle, it will die of starvation.

"So when you get up, if you are a gazelle, you'd better be running fast or you'll be the lion's dish. It is survival of the fittest. Usually we don't see lions eating the first gazelle or the ones in the middle of the pack. It's the ones who are last," Ted smiles.

While some may look at that proverb and be concerned for the poor gazelle, Ted looks at it as a phrase that also applies to everyday life and the pursuit of excellence. Again, hard work is essential to beat the lion.

"We compete in school, at work, in the business world and even in our personal lives. We can be eaten by poverty or our competitors. If we don't strive for our goals, we may be alive but we may be miserable for the rest of our lives."

* * *

As a young athlete in Africa, Ted learned better eating habits from his family and culture than those that exist in North America. "The kind of food we eat here is totally different. There was no such thing as junk food growing up in our culture. The healthier diet helped to increase our performance levels."

Many people in Regina have commented on how skinny Ted is. Even Ted's sister mentioned it when he went back for his first visit in 1999. The over-indulgent North American culture was not being very kind to her brother, she thought. She would not accept Ted's explanation that "all runners are skinny." She fed him three meals a day and snacks to try to help him gain weight.

North Americans usually weigh themselves on a small scale they have in their own homes, but that situation is rare in Ethiopia. There, a person who wants to be weighed must pay a merchant in the marketplace and step on a scale that would normally be used to weigh coffee or grain.

To make his sister happy, Ted weighed himself on a scale in the open market. The scale said he had gained three kilograms after a few weeks of eating her food, which she was delighted to hear. The scales there were wrong, though. When Ted got back to Canada, he found that he had actually lost four kilograms (about eight pounds).

"The food there is more homegrown, more veggie-based. There is no fried food, no junk food. My energy level was high when I came back. I felt so great. Here, we have chocolate bars, chips and soda drinks every day. We don't consume large quantities of soft drinks in Ethiopia like some people do here." A 355-millilitre can of pop, the most common size sold in Canada, contains about 40 grams of sugar, which is more than 13 teaspoons of sugar.

Ted has always been careful with his own diet, out of necessity when he was in exile and struggling to earn an income in his early days in Canada, but mostly for his athletic requirements. He encourages North Americans of all ages to get more active by doing some type of exercising, but he notes that daily exercise alone is not enough.

"You have to watch what you put in your mouth." Ted, for example, needs more calories for energy when he is competing and reduces his calorie intake the rest of the time. He doesn't consume a lot of alcohol and doesn't eat a lot of junk food or sweet desserts. "Usually bad food tastes great. It's not necessarily good for us, but we tend to like it."

A lot of the meals Ted cooks at home consist of either rice or pasta. He often cooks a large batch of pasta sauce to freeze individual portions for later meals. He likes barbecued hamburger, roast beef and beef stew, but his favourite meat is roast or broiled chicken. He does not eat large portions and rarely eats dessert.

When he was young, dessert was usually fruit. Now, he not only avoids dessert because of his running, he isn't really interested in it. "I don't have any urge or desire to eat cake or ice cream. When friends come for supper, sometimes they are waiting for dessert and I have to say: 'No, guys. No dessert. If you want dessert, you have to go out.' My son doesn't like my cooking. He finds it too simple."

Adam admits that he would prefer something a little spicier or would at least like to have some variety in his meals. "My dad would eat rice every single day."

Ted blames the North American consumer-based culture for the increase in obesity among children and adults. "The fast-food industry advertises their products on TV all the time. Many fast foods have high-sugar and high-fat content. The availability of that food, our lack of self-control and our fast-paced lifestyle are responsible for the epidemic obesity problem we have here."

Statistics show that during the past 25 years, obesity rates have risen for all adult age groups except those 65 and older. In 1978/79, 3% of children aged 2 to 17 were obese. By 2004, that number had more than doubled to 8%. Among adults, the growth in obesity went from 14% to 23% in 25 years. Now, one in four Canadian adults is considered obese.[28]

People who eat fruits and vegetables five or more times a day are much less likely to be overweight or obese than those who eat them less often. Spending more hours watching TV, playing video games or using the computer contribute to a more sedentary lifestyle, which also increases the likelihood of obesity.[29]

It comes down to the individual, says Ted. "We must restrain ourselves. We must have self-control. Nobody will look after us. We must be responsible for our actions in everyday life, including what we eat and what we do," he insists.

"Fitness is a lifetime commitment. It is an investment in your future. I have seen a few people start to exercise only when things go wrong with their health later in life rather than taking preventive measures with their health when they are younger."

Ted knows that not everyone strives to be a competitive runner like him, and he acknowledges that competition at that level is not the goal. "Make some time to exercise now and build a solid base for your own good health. Fitness is very important."

He notes that one of the more fulfilling aspects of his coaching is watching how the pursuit of fitness makes a positive difference in people's lives. "To see inactive people grow to be self-confident achievers is marvelous."

* * *

Ted is a reluctant hero. He is a passionate role model who does not run or coach for the gratitude that might come from it. He does these things because he believes he can help others improve their own lives. He leads by example.

A 2006 thank-you card from the university athletes he coaches contained many heartfelt handwritten messages of appreciation for his efforts in the past year. Although a bit overstated and with a hint of teasing, one message speaks volumes of the respect the athletes have for their coach. "You are the Messiah," says the notation. "We will be champions because of you."

Terry Mountjoy, a founding member of Regina Wheat City Kinsmen Track and Field Club which is now called Excel Athletika, looks out the window of his office and marvels at what Ted has been able to accomplish as a runner and coach during the past 20 years. "We cannot separate people from their culture. When you look at people who are very successful, it's because they have been able to draw on those positive things about their culture but also the negative things, and been able to overcome those to become stronger. I think we see that in Ted. In athletics, you have to overcome opposition in the people you're competing against. Recognizing that creates strength in people. Very few people are able to be successful in anything in life if it comes too easily."

Chapter Thirteen

An Honourable Future

In 2005, two of Ted's adult student athletes paid their coach the ultimate compliment. They nominated him to the Saskatchewan Sports Hall of Fame and Museum.

"Running has been as integral to Ted as breathing, and his story is a breathtaking, inspirational and sometimes poignant reminder, to those of us striving in athletics, of the true meaning of determination," says the form that Chris Vuksic and Jill Rodgers filled out to request that Ted be inducted into the Hall of Fame.

"He has made an indelible mark in Canadian and international distance running... Perhaps, more importantly, his name is known by runners and athletes throughout the province. If one stops any runner on the river path in Saskatoon or Wascana Park in Regina, they will all know the name Ted Jaleta, and usually will tell a story of how he has personally inspired them." The form goes on to note that Ted stays in top shape and still participates in local road races during the summer months, "running spectacular times seemingly effortlessly... Throughout his lifetime Ted Jaleta continues to define for Saskatchewan what it is to be an athlete."

Rodgers, an employee and family assistance counsellor, ran her first marathon in the fall of 2000 and was introduced by Ted to Vuksic. The women became training partners and rivals in many of the Timex Road Race series Masters events over the next few years. Rodgers says it was only logical to nominate Ted for the Sports Hall of Fame. "We wanted to have a way to honour him and showcase to the community what kind of athlete and coach he is. It's quite amazing having someone of his level in Regina."

"He is absolutely inspiring to all of us," adds Vuksic. "Ted has turned defeat into victory."

A nominee to the Saskatchewan Sports Hall of Fame and Museum must be someone who has represented sport with distinction or brought great credit to sport and been retired from competing in their sport for at least three years, among having other credentials. It was obvious to Vuksic and Rodgers that Ted fulfilled the criteria, but the decision wasn't quite as easy for the committee that reviewed the nominations.

There was considerable discussion of Ted's appropriateness for the Sports Hall of Fame, says executive director Sheila Kelly. "Ted is very unique for us because his athletic career is not necessarily one rooted in any of the major games, so when our selection committee was reviewing the nominations, the first reaction was: 'He's a Masters athlete.' We don't go out of our way to recognize a Masters athlete."

Most athletes inducted into the Saskatchewan Sports Hall have had strong junior careers and then gone on to a higher level of sport. Ted did not have that early background in Saskatchewan. Still, there was much about him that persuaded the committee members to take a closer look.

"Our process is that we accept nominations from the public. We ask for a nominee's entire history on the local, provincial and national scene," explains Kelly. "Ted's a little bit different. He has certainly had a great deal of success in the events in Saskatchewan. He's given back incredibly to the Saskatchewan community. One of the items that really struck us was the fact he was ranked seventh in the world as a long distance runner at the Masters level. That did really stick with us."

The selection committee further examined Ted's history and accomplishments and came away fully impressed. "Ted's life and all of the exploits that had happened in his life really took on a great deal of significance and added to the push to have him installed in the Sports Hall of Fame," adds Kelly. The committee approved the induction and began finding out more about him to include in his display that would have a place of honour in the downtown Regina museum for the first year after his induction. A plaque would commemorate his induction thereafter.

"It was just such a wonderful journey that we all took with Ted," Kelly says. "He has been inducted as an athlete into our hall but he is such a builder of the sport. So many of the people we have come to know through his induction are essentially his students he has coached."

At a ceremony held on the evening of June 11, 2005, Ted was officially inducted into the Saskatchewan Sports Hall of Fame. He became the first African-born person to have that honour.

There were 800 people at the banquet that night at the Centre of the Arts, listening intently to former National Hockey League goaltender Ed Staniowski, who played with the Regina Pats, accept the honours on behalf of the inductees. Ted and Staniowski joined an illustrious group of more than 300 individual recipients and 60 teams inducted into the Hall of Fame, including Saskatchewan Roughriders fullback George Reed, Olympic runner Lynn (Kanuka) Williams, Olympic pentathlete Diane Jones Konihowski, and the Sandra Schmirler Curling Team.

"We have inductees who have joined us from Iron Curtain countries," says Kelly. "What makes Ted unique, to the best of my knowledge, is we have nobody who has literally escaped with their life and started over and done that with such success."

She added that, as anyone who knows Ted might expect, he has since gone above and beyond the usual to show his appreciation for the award. "What we really like about Ted is, now that he has been honoured and is one of ours, he certainly has embraced the sense of ownership in the Hall. He's willing to get involved and give back. We've recognized him and he really feels he has a certain debt to us."

Since the induction ceremony, Ted has volunteered for various awareness-raising and fundraising events for the Saskatchewan Sports Hall of Fame and Museum, to support the organization that honoured him. "He's eternally grateful for everything that he has," says Kelly. "He's been through the worst the world has to offer and he sees what Canada has to offer. He's so wanting to appreciate that and not to exploit it."

During a later visit to the Hall of Fame museum, Ted asked if an individual could be inducted as both an athlete and a builder in the same sport. The answer was no. Only one award per person per sport. He was told he would have to find a new sport if he wanted to be inducted again. So he jokingly said maybe he should take up curling and become the first black curler to be inducted into the Saskatchewan Sports Hall. The other person said to him: "You know, just stay with your running. It will take you until you're 80 years old to be any good at curling."

As part of the display for the Hall of Fame award, Ted was asked to reflect on his achievements in sport and how sport has affected his personal life and career. "I used running as a vehicle to enhance both my personal and professional life," he said in the display materials. "It gave me a sense of structure, which allowed me to stabilize my life and give back to the society that had provided me a new home and country."

He added that sports gave him a way to free himself from the negative things around him and taught him the commitment and dedication required to excel in everyday life. "Lessons I learned from sport have taught me to set goals and achieve them through personal commitments."

Sitting at the dinner table that night during the induction ceremonies was one of the most amazing moments of Ted's life. Yet his mind was a swirl of emotions. He was pleased and excited and sad and confused, in disbelief and at times totally overwhelmed that his name and portrait would be permanently displayed on the wall beside other great athletes and builders of sport in Saskatchewan.

It didn't seem that long ago when he looked out his apartment window and wondered if a quick run in the park might help him to feel better about himself as a new resident of Canada. Now, he was here, listening to the accolades. It was hard to believe.

"It was a great night. To be recognized in front of my peer groups was wonderful," he says. Still, he felt a bit lost.

His son Adam was beside him and many good friends were all around, but at that moment, Ted dearly missed his family in Ethiopia. He wished his parents could have seen how far he had come since he ran away from home all those years ago. They had never seen him run, in Ethiopia or in Canada.

"Here I was, sitting at the Hall of Fame dinner... They would have enjoyed seeing that. Most of the inductees were sitting with their parents. I didn't have any."

Ted's Canadian mom was planning to fly in from British Columbia but a good friend was terminally ill and she had to stay to take care of her. Ted was glad that Adam was there and he knew his son was proud of him that night. "Maybe my parents were watching me that night from above. I hope they were. I know they would have been proud of me."

Several times throughout the evening, Ted felt like he was in a dream. "I couldn't believe this was happening. It was a miracle. Compared to 27 years ago, when I was sitting at the refugee camp, I never imagined the broken pieces of my life would be back together and so perfect like this. It was a great time."

Ted also knew that this event marked a historic point in his life. He thought to himself this was the highest achievement he could have in his athletic career. That night, a chapter of his life came to a close. He had to move on to other things.

One of the lasting memories Ted has from the Sports Hall of Fame induction evening came from an incident that occurred after the formal presentations were made. A man who had known him when Ted first arrived in Regina walked up and congratulated him. He asked for Ted's autograph and said he couldn't believe that Ted had reached this height of achievement. Although the man didn't say much more, Ted knew there was something else that remained unspoken.

"I sensed that he seemed remorseful for not believing in me in those early years. He didn't apologize or say anything else, but I knew what he wanted to say."

That brief interaction came at a perfect time in Ted's life. He had come so far since he stepped off that plane in Regina in 1982. People all around him had finally recognized his gifts and abilities, and who he was as an individual.

His brush with his past on this night reaffirmed he had been walking the right path all along. Ted also knew for sure that his dream of achieving success as a runner had finally become a reality.

* * *

Sitting at home on the night of the Hall of Fame induction dinner, Fay Burton was thinking of her 'proxy son.' "He is so worthy of any complement," she gushes like a proud mother. "Being inducted into the Sports Halls of Fame for Saskatchewan, that is so great. He just deserves everything that he gets. He has come through a horrendous ordeal to get here in the first place. We don't see young Canadians with as much glue, as much fibre, as you see with Ted. Our fellows don't know hardships," she says of her own sons. "They don't know what it's like to starve."

Burton had sent Ted an e-mail more than two years earlier, on February 11, 2003. In it, she referred to a speech Ted had recently made to a Saskatchewan audience, but her comments could have easily been read to him at the Sports Hall of Fame induction and applied that night:

"What can I say to you and about you that hasn't already been said in praise?" she wrote in the 2003 e-mail. "Thanks for sending us a copy of a wonderful account of your struggles on the road to achieving the present level of success and respect you enjoy, and so rightly deserve today. As I read your speech, the part where you mention having to give up your dream of an Olympic medal brought a different take to my mind... Ted, a medal is a metal symbol acknowledging, for the most part, a person's athletic ability... something worn around one's neck on special occasions... The 'medal' you possess is etched in your mind, heart and soul to be felt and shared with everyone who comes in contact with you," wrote Burton.

"It is like the eternal flame... It never goes out or stops radiating from you...As long as you live, you, in person, will be that symbol that people can hear and see...That living example of what one can be with sheer strength and determination, principles and faith in God... In other words, you are a walking gold medal."

She summed up her letter by saying: "You will likely never know how proud I am to be your friend... your proxy mom."

Ted has cherished that piece of correspondence, for good reason, ever since.

* * *

Since his arrival in Canada in 1982, Ted has spent countless volunteer hours assisting new immigrants and refugees, particularly those from African countries, and offering advice on how they can successfully integrate into Canadian society. He shares his experiences and recommends what they need to adapt to this new world. He tells them how the Canadian system works and what opportunities are available to them.

"Over the years, Ted has become a role model for the African community in Regina," says Darren Burrows. "When there are new Africans coming to town, Ted tries to communicate with them and tells them: 'Don't do that. Don't get involved in this.' He tries to help them integrate successfully."

Ted's assistance has extended into his international running circles as well. African-born runners called him 'Mzee,' the Swahili word for 'wise man' and a term of respect for those older than oneself. "Some of these international runners would look to Ted to help them, because some agents in the road race circuit would try to take advantage of the African runners," says Burrows. "The runners communicate. A lot of them would talk to Ted about whether or not they were being taken advantage of."

One of Ted's friends within the Ethiopian community in Regina has called him 'a rare breed' for his ability to ignore political and ethnic lines that may have separated today's refugees if they were in Ethiopia. Ted is well-respected among the 50 or so former Ethiopians living in Regina and has had some success in his efforts to bring people together, as his namesake Emperor Tewodros II did generations ago.

An Ethiopian pavilion held during the 2006 Mosaic multicultural fair in Regina is an example of the work done by Ted and several other members of the local Ethiopian Association to unite the community towards a common goal. The three-day event featured performances by about 20 dancers of all ages plus samples of traditional Ethiopian food, bamboo weaving, crafts and traditional clothing. Visitors could also taste coffee from Ethiopia and learn more about that country's culture during a traditional coffee ceremony.

Ted is actively involved in the Ethiopian Association, which provides emotional and community support to ease the transition for newcomers to Regina, including a university student who recently arrived from the same region where Ted was born. Ted is also the treasurer of the association's Amharic School, which teaches the Amharic language to children and others who are interested. The association's focus is on improving the lives of those in Regina. "We don't allow any political issue to be on the agenda. We are teaching them to get rid of whatever baggage they brought with them. This is a community to help each other and expose Ethiopian culture to Canadians."

Ted has also volunteered for years, through a Canada Revenue Agency program, to help low-income individuals and immigrants fill out their income tax forms.

His attitude to charitable work was something he learned from his mother. "My mom was a very generous, caring person and she taught us it was okay to give our free time to others. She always told us: 'Don't do it to be noticed. Do it because you love it.' Whatever experience you have, share it with someone in a positive manner."

Ted is an eclectic music lover with diverse musical tastes ranging from classical to the more contemporary tunes on the radio. He enjoys the music of African a capella group Ladysmith Black Mambazo and American soprano Renée Fleming. Ted listens to the blues music of BB King and others to relax, and says he can understand the pain of those who created these songs of agony and freedom so many years ago.

He also listens to opera, finding he can relate to the traditional themes of tragedy and sadness. He doesn't understand the language but reads the written descriptions and appreciates the rich, beautiful voices.

Ted regularly attends performances of the Regina Symphony Orchestra and assists that organization as a guest celebrity at various fundraisers. One glimpse of dark-skinned Ted in a white wig, tuxedo jacket and shorts while running in the 'Beat Beethoven' charity race is enough to spur even the stingiest person to ante up donations to the Regina Symphony Orchestra and Regina Qu'Appelle Health Region. The goal is to run the eight-kilometre course in the time it takes to play Beethoven's 9th Symphony, which is just under 50 minutes. Ted always finishes well before the 30-minute mark.

Ted officiated at Western Canada Summer Games 1989 track events and was a diversity ambassador at Canada Summer Games 2005, representing the Multicultural Council of Saskatchewan. "Diversity makes us stronger as a city, a province and as a nation," he said at the time. "The Canadian mosaic includes Aboriginal people, visible minorities, multicultural communities and others. All of these people have talent, energy and enthusiasm to contribute. All have a role in making Canada stronger."

During a 2006 Saskatchewan Athletics High School track meet in Moose Jaw, Ted showed yet again why he is so revered in the community. At the event, Ted met a teenaged boy from Sudan who was an excellent runner and had earned medals in the 400 metres. The boy had recently arrived in Saskatchewan and was staying with a host family. He did not have proper running attire.

So on the second day of the track meet, Ted arrived carrying a bag full of his own extra shoes and track suits for this newcomer to Canada. Ted watched as tears of gratitude welled up in the young boy's eyes and remembered his own early days of running in Canada.

"I gave him encouragement and I told him I was once in the same situation. And I gave him my phone number and told him to phone me any time."

Yes, Ted had been in that young boy's position once, with tons of ability and little else. He had also moved well past that place, largely on his own. It was only natural that the grown man, a now-respected athlete and leader, would help someone else to move forward and use his own talents to build a better life.

* * *

In the mid 1990s, Ted began getting requests to do some public speaking at schools and other venues. He has since addressed numerous elementary and high school gatherings about the importance of education, fitness and a positive attitude. He has a particular fondness for inner-city schools, which have a higher population of students from low-income families. He also talks to community and sports groups about the importance of fitness, wellness and mentoring.

Among his more memorable speaking engagements was being the special guest at an anti-racism day in a Regina elementary school, and speaking to a church group that was raising funds to bring a refugee family to Canada. He also addressed a Canada Revenue Agency regional managers' forum, where his then-workplace supervisor Dave Marshall says Ted's story hit the mark. "His message of 'Don't give up hope,' and the struggles he had either with our climate or the language were very well received," says Marshall.

He remembers going to the Regina Fieldhouse during the winter to exercise and seeing Ted there working with his student athletes. "The kids would come up to me and say: 'Oh, do you know Ted? What a nice guy he is. He sure helped me with my running.'"

Marshall also recalls a situation a few years ago when Canada Revenue Agency workers were picketing in front of the building. "Ted found that very difficult because it reminded him of the protest in Ethiopia. That brought back some bad memories for him. He was excused from picket duty."

Ted has learned and grown considerably since Marshall met him in the 1990s. "When I look at way back then, his command of the English language and where he is now, that's quite an accomplishment," says Marshall. "He was going to university and is still continuing to learn. Now he's taking accounting classes after work that our office has sponsored. He's still very humble. He's brought a different perspective to our work environment. We offer courses on diversity here, but Ted's a pretty good example of that."

In October 2005, Ted was invited by Tracy Bourne to speak to a group of teenagers who had been in trouble with the law. Bourne is a top long distance runner and coach in Saskatchewan who works as a counsellor for youth in custody at Orcadia Youth Residence in Yorkton, about 190 kilometres northeast of Regina. She had met Ted a year earlier near the starting line of a 10K race in Regina.

"I remember feeling apprehensive and insecure during this

introduction because I was certain that an athlete of his ability wouldn't be very interested in an unknown like myself," explains Bourne. "Ted however walked up, shook my hand, posed several questions, included me in the warm-up and steered me to the start line with encouraging words for the race. It is this genuine interest in the well-being of others that makes Ted such an amazing person."

Bourne thought that Ted's story of overcoming the adversities in his life might have a positive effect on the youth at Orcadia who face challenges that sometimes seem insurmountable. "I have seen youth who have given up and those who believe that their lives cannot improve, so they do not challenge themselves to make a difference," she says.

That was before Ted walked in, told his story and got through to his audience.

"He gave a very moving and motivational speech that had lasting effects on these kids. He reached them. When he started talking, he was so genuine and emotional. He broke down, and for the kids to see someone become that vulnerable and exposed about his life and his experiences, it allowed them to see it is okay. They saw that some people have been dealt a hand worse off than what they've been dealt, and can still be a success."

The youth wrote letters of thanks to Ted after his speech. One said he lifted her out of the pit of gloom. "I had a troubling time growing up, but nothing like yours, and I still dwell on the past and live in self-pity," she wrote. "After hearing your story, you made me think about what I want. Because of your story, you made me believe I can succeed and become stronger from my past."

Another youth learned appreciation for the good life that Canada has to offer and that his life was a lot more peaceful than he ever thought. "My thought on him is that he lived two lives, one full of turmoil, poverty and starvation. His second life was one with food, work, education, friends and opportunities," wrote the youth.

Still another talked about gaining a new understanding of name-calling and individual gifts. "When you told us about when people thought you were stupid and you started to cry, I felt sorry for you… I just thought you must have been through a lot of stuff and abuse. And the good thing is you never gave up, you just kept going. And look where you're at now. You're not stupid and you have a good talent in running and you're not wasting it. And I learned if you grew up in a bad place, that doesn't mean you can't do something with your life. You gotta just keep going."

Bourne will always remember the looks on the faces of the youth as they heard Ted's story that day. "Many people spend too much time searching for ways to make themselves happy," she says. "Ted has earned respect, trust and friendship through making others happy. He is a natural leader, a powerful role model and an extraordinary friend. We need a lot more people like Ted Jaleta in the world."

Daphne Bilokury, a runner who is a manager with Canada Life in Regina, met Ted when she and her running partner asked him for tips to improve their qualifying times for the Boston Marathon. They were surprised that Ted immediately invited them to the Douglas Park track that same week. Bilokury later asked Ted to make a presentation on wellness and positive thinking to a group of insurance company workers. In his speech, he talked about goal setting, aspirations and overcoming adversity.

"He was very professional. He did a great job speaking about his life and the things he has overcome, and he talked about well-being as a person. No matter what happens in your life, if you are healthy and happy, you can overcome almost anything," recalls Bilokury.

"Do not get consumed by negative things around you," Ted told the Canada Life staff that day. "You are in a position to affect others at work and in the community. You can create change for the good of others."

He encouraged them to take the time to add exercise and nutrition to their lives. "Give yourself that gift without feeling selfish or guilty. Even a half-hour walk a few times a week will help," he said. "Once you make the time in your life for wellness, it will become routine. When you feel better about yourself, you make others around you feel better, you are more productive at work and home, and you are just a better person all around," he said.

"I learned long ago not to measure success by the material comforts we are able to afford. I advised my son not to make money the goal but, instead, to pursue the things he loves and to do them well. I told him he may encounter many defeats, but he must not be defeated. My early upbringing has groomed me to always look at the long-term results rather than looking for quick successes."

Ted added: "It's all about believing in yourself and that you can do more than you realize. It takes hard work and discipline, but do not give up. Be resilient. You have already achieved great careers and lives for yourselves. You can be role models out there and can make a difference for others. Anything is possible if you focus on your gifts and use them to help others. We all want to leave a positive legacy. Positive choices equals success."

Then he left them with six concepts that he believes are positive choices for a better world:

Appreciate all that you are and all that you have. "I believe all human beings have kindness in them. We should appreciate our loved ones and those around us. Each of us has gifts and talents and we should make use of them. We are so occupied with material interests. A lot of people think they don't have enough and they put a lot of stress on themselves to acquire more. We should be grateful for what we have, especially good health, and what this country has to offer."

Take advantage of worthwhile opportunities. "In this country, you can be anything you want. The question is: Are you willing to work for it? I encourage you to take advantage of learning options and take a risk that might lead to a better future. Don't let your fears hold you back. In the end, it will enhance your life."

Make goals and alternative goals. "Setting short-term and long-term goals can provide a sense of direction and purpose to accomplish results. Meaningful goals lead to gratification of our efforts and provide a more structured life. The key is to use our time effectively to do the work."

Mental fitness is as important as physical fitness. "Look after your mind and your body. Regular exercise will improve your physical and mental condition. An attitude of life-long learning will help us grow as individuals. Education provides freedom, power and financial reward. Education and physical fitness together provide a winning formula leading to a better quality of life."

Be aware of and avoid things that will play a destructive role in your life. "We are all faced with good and bad choices. We need to analyze them closely. My advice is to avoid drugs and other negative factors that tend to hold people back in their lives. Also think about where you spend your time. Choose friends who will be a positive influence in your life and don't be deterred by negativity around you. Believe in your dreams and strive to live your life to the fullest. You are responsible for your own life and actions. Ultimately, the solution is you."

Be ready to face the challenges that will surprise you. "Life is a bumpy road, whether you are rich, poor or in between. A broken relationship, death in the family or job loss can be devastating. Take advantage of resources that are around you. Difficult times often help us grow as individuals to become better persons. Be aware that there will be roadblocks on your journey. Accept defeat as a learning experience and not as a failure, so you can later return to a positive, healthy state of mind."

* * *

From the Ethiopian Highlands to his new life in Canada, Ted has run on one of the roughest roads life could have set for him, with obstacles obscuring his vision at every turn. He has faced the challenges on the journey with incredible courage, grace, determination and humility, seeking to improve the lives of others along the way. His is a life of victory, rich with hope and possibilities. He is truly an inspiration, encouraging all to live their lives to the fullest.

Epilogue

In 2006 at age 51, Ted Jaleta is still running strong in Saskatchewan races. He finished third in the 21.1K Regina Police Half Marathon, losing to two of his athletes, whom he teased were being "disrespectful" by beating their coach. He came in first overall in the SGI Canada Charity 10K Road Race and finished only two seconds behind 33-year-old Jason Warick in the 10K Sweetheart Run Walk and Roll in Regina. In the Saskatoon Half Marathon, Ted came in third overall.

In May 2006, he also achieved his 11th victory in the Fort Qu'Appelle/ Echo Lake Road Race, which he has only entered 13 times since 1986. He finished a full four metres in front of his nearest competitor in 2006, an incredible feat for a runner of his age.

"When I first came to Canada more than 20 years ago, the people who knew me then and know me now say I am a totally different person now. Back then, I was unable to open up and trust others. Now, I know my surroundings and I am more comfortable. I am now willing to talk about my past and I find it helps when I share my experiences. It is a healing process for me."

Ted speaks highly of Bono, lead singer of the Irish rock band U2, who uses his celebrity status to fight poverty in developing countries. Ted's status as a well-respected athlete in his own community is now allowing him to get his own humanitarian message across.

"I don't know what the future holds for me. I didn't know if I would even be alive, never mind to have all these good things happen." Ted wants to use running to share his positive message with people who would like to hear it. He wants to share his experiences of adversity to encourage others to not give up and to move towards a life of success and happiness for themselves.

"If it wasn't for running, nobody would listen to my message."

Ted knows that he is not the only refugee who has suffered atrocities. He has simply made it to a level that allows him to share his wisdom with others.

He worries that many refugees in Canada and elsewhere may not be coping well from the trauma they've experienced. "They are still crying inside and keeping it to themselves." Ted has learned that it helps to talk about it, and he will continue to do so as long as someone will listen.

He has no regrets about the way he has lived his life so far since being in Canada. "The last 20 years here have been wonderful. I have lived my life here to the fullest. I had to regroup and re-establish to become a productive member of society and be in the position to help others. I am now able to influence people and help my family here and in Africa."

He also helped Jason Warick raise money to help build a much-needed high school for orphans in Kenya. Ted recruited a dozen or more volunteers to prepare food, sell juice and silent auction items, as well as play African music at a fundraising event. He quoted from the great African leader Nelson Mandela that night, saying: 'Education is the most powerful weapon which you can use to change the world.' About $5,000 was raised for the high school and 500 pairs of running shoes were also sent to Africa as part of that promotion.

"These donations can make a huge difference toward providing basic education that is the cornerstone for self-sufficiency and freedom from poverty," Ted told the audience that night. "Your donations will especially help to minimize the gender inequality that exists between boys and girls. Your donations will broaden the opportunities available for young women in both their business and professional lives."

He talked about helping people to recognize and pursue the key ingredients to a good life. "Through perseverance, dedication to hard work and believing in yourself, you will reap many rewards. It's all about the right choices. In this country, you have the opportunity to be anything you want to be. Let's share that dream with those of other nations, and help them to have the best of both worlds in education and sports."

These days, Ted can often be found talking to students in schools or on the track, encouraging them to get an education, to figure out what they are meant to be doing in their lives, and to work towards their dreams.

The young ones sit wide-eyed as he briefly outlines his experiences in Africa, from running happily alongside monkeys to sitting on a dirt floor in school, then begging for food in a refugee camp. They run up to him after his speeches to ask for his autograph and a hug. Ted graciously and gratefully hands out both, hoping his message will inspire these youngsters to achieve success and be able to surpass the obstacles they will surely encounter.

He talks to business and community leaders about using their skills for the betterment of society. He tells them they are privileged compared to the adults in most of the countries of the world, and he encourages them to use their powers in a positive way to motivate and inspire their staff.

His message of struggle, courage and hope sometimes reduces both himself and his audience members to tears. It is still so real.

Ted continues to share his money with people in Africa and he has lived simply for years in an apartment that most North Americans would consider small. For him, it is enough. He has other priorities.

Ted's refrigerator door is decorated with photos of the two most important people in his life, his son Adam and Olympic champion Abebe Bikila. Another sheet of paper on the fridge door displays Ted's favourite quote from Irish writer George Bernard Shaw: 'I want to be thoroughly used up when I die. For the harder I work, the more I live. Life is a sort of splendid torch which I have got hold of for a moment, and I want to make it burn as brightly as possible before handing it on to future generations.'

The famous quote from Shaw could easily be Ted's motto. He has been living hard and working hard throughout his life. He has carried a splendid torch and has shared that flame generously and gratefully.

"We have the power to steer our lives in a positive direction by recognizing our gifts, setting goals and believing in ourselves. Sometimes our path may not be as smooth as we would like, but by approaching these bumps as learning opportunities for growth, our coping mechanism will improve. At times it may seem impossible to succeed but if one hangs in there through the adversity, personal growth will take over and a much richer, stronger person results. My advice to you is to believe in yourself and have faith in your gifts. Try to discover what it is that you are meant to be. Look for things that make your heart soar – times when you know you are doing absolutely the right thing."

'Follow your dreams,' advises Tewodros Jaleta.

He did.

Notes

Chapter One:	Page 16	1. Ethiopia: Transition and Development in the Horn of Africa; Mulatu Wubneh and Yohannis Abate; C. 1988 Westview Press Inc.
Chapter Two:	Page 18	2. Ethiopia; Carol Ann Gillespie; C. 2003 Chelsea House Publishers
	Page 30	3. Ethiopia; Carol Ann Gillespie; C. 2003 Chelsea House Publishers
Chapter Three:	Page 34	4, 5, 6. Ethiopia: Transition and Development in the Horn of Africa; Mulatu Wubneh and Yohannis Abate; C. 1988 Westview Press Inc. 7. Wikipedia, the Free Encyclopedia; www.wikipedia.org
	Page 36	8. Wikipedia, the Free Encyclopedia; www.wikipedia.org 9. Ethiopia; Carol Ann Gillespie; C. 2003 Chelsea House Publishers
	Page 37	10, 11. Wikipedia, the Free Encyclopedia; www.wikipedia.org 12. Ethiopia: Transition and Development in the Horn of Africa; Mulatu Wubneh and Yohannis Abate; C. 1988 Westview Press Inc.
	Page 38	13. Ethiopia: Transition and Development in the Horn of Africa; Mulatu Wubneh and Yohannis Abate; C. 1988 Westview Press Inc.
Chapter Four:	Page 50	14. Wikipedia, the Free Encyclopedia; www.wikipedia.org
Chapter Five:	Page 57	15. Ethiopia; Carol Ann Gillespie; C. 2003 Chelsea House Publishers
Chapter Six:	Page 62	16. Wikipedia, the Free Encyclopedia - www.wikipedia.org
	Page 67	17. Canadian Council for Refugees: A Hundred Years of Immigration to Canada, 1900-1999; www.web.net/~ccr/history.html
Chapter Seven:	Page 78	18. City of Regina; www.regina.ca 19. Wascana Centre; www.wascana.sk.ca
Chapter Nine:	Page 104	20. Regina Leader-Post; May 24, 1988.
	Page 115	21, 22. Regina Leader-Post; May 14, 1995. 23. Regina Leader-Post; May 11, 1996.
Chapter Ten:	Page 117	24. University of Wyoming; Athletics Hall of Fame 1997; http://wyomingathletics.cstv.com
	Page 118	25. Wikipedia, the Free Encyclopedia; www.wikipedia.org
	Page 119	26. Regina Leader-Post; October 23, 1996
Chapter Twelve:	Page 133	27. Regina Leader-Post; September 13, 2000
	Page 148	28, 29. Canadian Community Health Survey: Obesity among children and adults; 2004

A Final Word From Ted

More than 10 years ago, I was first approached to tell my life story in the form of a book. A few years later, someone asked me if they could produce a film documentary on my life. I didn't take them seriously at the time. I never thought anyone would care about it and I didn't want to revisit the negative experiences or have that as the focus of my life story.

When I started talking to groups in the early 1990s about some of the details of my life, people in the audience told me they were fascinated and wanted to hear more and more. They were learning from my story and asked me to consider sharing this information. Then I met Peggy Collins in the late 1990s and she believed that I should share my story with a larger audience. She assisted me in the process of creating motivational talks. Without her efforts, this book would not have been published.

Thank you to Peggy and Deana for helping me to tell my story. They have put in many hours and have put up with my moments of stress. It has been intense but it has been a blessing. I have grown and learned a lot. I am still learning new skills and am enjoying finding people in Canada who will put up with me.

I want to say a special thank you to the Burton and Bolstad families for helping me in my early days in Canada, and to the Vuksic family and Marion Craig for their support in the later years. They welcomed me into their homes and families and taught me many social skills for my new life in Canada. They were patient with me and gave me their unconditional love and support. We have shared many good times and lots of laughter. I remember in those early years that I sometimes did not understand what they were saying, but I nodded my head anyways.

Thank you to Darren Burrows, Jason Warick, John Bolstad, Rob McKechney and others who were the significant individuals who accepted me with open arms through their love of running and sense of humour. Even though they have said so many good things about me in this book without me paying them, the feeling is mutual. When I needed someone to listen to my pains and triumphs, they are the ones I trusted. They accepted me, even though I am older than they are, when I was just starting my life in Canada. They taught me how the Canadian system and culture work and they made my transition into Canadian society easier when I was receiving mixed signals from others. The lessons I have learned from all these people are greater than what I ever shared with them.

The arrival of my son Adam gave me a sense of hope and stability. He gave me a purpose to live and I am blessed to have him. I can't imagine my life without him. Thank you, Adam.

Thank you to my managers and co-workers at Canada Revenue Agency who have supported me and encouraged me to fulfill my passion for running and helping others. I am grateful they believed in me. Thank you to Jill Rodgers and Chris Vuksic for nominating me to the Saskatchewan Sports Hall of Fame. They believed that I was worthy of that recognition and I am grateful.

My family in Ethiopia endured much difficulty because of me. I hope it is a blessing for my family that I have been able to survive and share my experiences with others. I regret that not all of them were able to witness the positive results of my life. I have dedicated this book to my sister Sadate, but I honour all of them with my story.

I am amazed at my life's journey to this point. It seems unbelievable to think that someone who was born in a remote Ethiopian village could drift to Canada, meet Peggy and Deana, and publish a book that could reach so many others.

I hope this book inspires you, our readers. If it helps one person to overcome some challenges or makes a difference for a few people, we will have reached our goal.

Acknowledgements: Peggy Collins

What a blessing it has been to be a part of Ted's life over the last seven years. I've always felt that Ted has a great message and purpose for this world. I admire him as a leader and feel proud to promote him as such in my work as a business and personal consultant.

Ted has not only recovered from unbelievable atrocities and excelled, but has actually used those negative experiences to his advantage. I do believe the key success factor here is listening to that internal voice, or intuition as some people call it, and following the opportunities provided for us. How many times do we wish we would have followed our intuition? How many opportunities have we missed? Ted was very decisive when these opportunities came along for him.

I would like to thank my family who has always supported me through the great adventures I seem to attract in my life. I would also like to thank my good friend, Rhonda Barry, who dreamed the dream along with me to bring hope to others through Ted's inspiring story. Your input was welcomed and greatly appreciated. I especially want to thank Ted for allowing me into his mind and his heart so that our shared vision could become a reality; and thank you to Deana for sharing her experience and knowledge.

As leader of this project, it has brought me great joy to guide its path and bring parties together to accomplish our goal: to inspire people to never give up and remember that there's always hope! We have learned so much from each other. Combining three heads has proven to be far better than anything each one of us could have created individually. I know we have all grown from this experience and are better people because of it. I hope you, too, find growth and peace from the words within this book.

ACKNOWLEDGEMENTS: DEANA DRIVER

While working on this book, I have often been astounded at the deep strength and wisdom that comes from within Ted Jaleta. Aside from being the excellent runner that he is, Ted is an intellectual, a philosopher, a humanitarian, a role model and leader. As you will have read, he is also a genuinely caring and decent human being who is reluctant to be called a 'hero.' That, of course, is why he deserves the honour.

I am grateful that Ted has had the courage to share his inspiring story of struggle, determination and hope. Many will benefit from this book including refugees to Canada, and teenagers and adults who need encouragement and strength. Ted's goals of education and excellence are worthy challenges for everyone. As an individual and a journalist, those have been my goals as well and they are the reasons I am honoured to now be part of Ted's story.

Thank you to our editorial panel of readers: Mary Harelkin Bishop, Dani Driver, Dave Driver and Jason Warick. Your keen eyes, enthusiasm and good advice helped immensely. Thank you also to Heather Nickel and Jeff DeDekker, our editors in the final stages. Thank you to Peggy for introducing me to Ted, for her vision and for the fun we've had since our first meeting. Thanks to Ted for being who he is to the world, for letting me into his head and for trusting me with his story.

Thank you to Al for always believing in me, to our three children and their partners, and to our family and friends who have supported me and cheered me on in this giant labour of love. Thanks especially to my parents, Alex and S. Agnes Pacholok, who never once tried to discourage me from my dream of being a journalist. Mom and Dad, this one's for you.

Never Give Up
TED JALETA'S INSPIRING STORY
by Deana Driver

LIMITED EDITION PRINTS
AS SEEN ON THE BACK COVER

CREATED FOR JDC PRODUCTIONS
BY TYSON KAKAKAWAY

$295.00 + TX + S&H

VISIT
www.tedjaleta.com

OR FILL OUT THE ORDER FORM
ON THE FOLLOWING PAGE

Never Give Up
TED JALETA'S INSPIRING STORY
by Deana Driver

LIMITED EDITION PRINTS ORDER FORM

NAME _____

ADDRESS _____

CITY _____

PROV/STATE _____

POSTAL/ZIP CODE _____

PHONE (   ) _____

EMAIL _____

___ PRINTS ORDERED @ $295.00 (+ TX + S&H)
(FOR SHIPPING COSTS, PHONE JDC PRODUCTIONS
OR VISIT WWW.TEDJALETA.COM)

PAID BY: MONEY ORDER ____   CHEQUE ____
(PAYABLE TO JDC PRODUCTIONS)

MAIL TO:

JDC PRODUCTIONS
3033 VICTORIA AVENUE
REGINA, SASKATCHEWAN, CANADA
S4T 1L1   (306-545-2448)